GROWTH TALK

A Coaching Way of Leading in Schools

"Got a minute? Because this is a book that shows educators how to lead not through directives and meetings, but through the kind of purposeful conversations that help people think better and do better."

—**Michael Bungay Stanier,** *The Coaching Habit*

Written by two leading authorities in the field of coaching in education, this book is an invaluable resource for leaders and educators who seek to inspire and motivate the people around them.

—**Christian van Nieuwerburgh**, bestselling author, executive coach, and educational consultant

At the heart of this book lies a deep belief in the infinite potential of people, particularly those who have committed their professional lives to schools and education. It offers a wonderful disconfirmation of the common belief that our leadership value lies in what we add. Instead, the invitation here is to create the conditions in which the greatness of others can emerge.

—**Penny Brown**, Leadership Centre, AISNSW

Munro and Campbell are deeply attuned, through their broad and deep experience, to the reality of the relational interactions at the heart of successful leadership and the time constraints therein.

—**Chris Browne**, principal, Kildare Catholic College

Munro and Campbell's book is a timely, uplifting guide for educational leaders seeking to transform hurried interactions into coachable moments.

—**Melanie Chambers**, British School of Brussels

This is the book I wish I had when I first became a middle leader; so many of my interactions and conversations would have benefited from the deliberate approach put forward in *Growth Talk*. The book not only ignites your passion for coaching and leading with a coaching approach but also provides granular steps and stems for conversations and dealing with situations.

—**Sam Crome**, director of education, Xavier Catholic Education Trust, England

Munro and Campbell masterfully show how every leader can shape culture, foster professional growth, build collective ownership, and improve outcomes—all through the quality of conversations we choose to have.

—**Adam Hogan**, principal in residence at the Victorian Academy of Teaching and Leadership

Educators who want to create and sustain dynamic, thriving, and growth-oriented relationships within their schools and school communities will find the resources and support to do so in *Growth Talk*. Munro and Campbell offer a book rich with examples, suggested approaches, and solid advice for transforming the way human beings work together and interact in schools. With the use of growth talk, adults and students can cultivate a learning environment grounded in the principles of honoring, trusting, and respecting one another and committing to each other's success.

—**Joellen Killion**, leadership and learning consultant

Growth Talk by Chris Munro and John Campbell is a must-read for anyone interested in coaching, in all its guises, in an educational context. What sets this book apart is its unique ability to engage the reader in an ongoing dialogue that not only inspires the cultivation of a coaching culture within and beyond their organisation but also equips them with powerful, accessible questions and prompts that help transform aspiration into action.

—**Joseph A. Moynihan**, former teacher and school principal, University College Cork (UCC) Ireland

The conversations that occur in schools are crucial to the goal of improving outcomes for students. Munro and Campbell provide the essentials of coaching conversations in a simple and practical guide that will support leaders at all levels to foster continuous growth and learning amongst their school communities. A great resource for fostering a culture of leading through purposeful conversations.

—**Kendra Parker**, director of Leadership Excellence Division, Victorian Academy of Teaching and Leadership

Practical, human, and full of heart, *Growth Talk* is the kind of book you want to hand to every leader, regardless of their role or industry. It's packed with clear, usable strategies that you can apply straight away, but what really stayed with me was the warmth and humility throughout. It's grounded, honest, and deeply respectful of what it means to lead with people in mind. A brilliant reminder that how we talk to each other really does shape the culture we build.

—**Carly Peart**, Bangkok Patana School

This book is as informative as it is practical—one to return to again and again. It powerfully reframes conversations not just as tools for reflection but as catalysts for growth in both learning and relationships. Most valuable for me was the insight into how consistent, quality conversations can shape a culture of learning across an entire organization—where everyone has the potential to lead through dialogue. A vital resource for those looking to not only build their own skills but to model coaching as a way of leading and learning.

—**Barbara Watterston**, CEO, Australian Council for Educational Leaders

GROWTH TALK

A Coaching Way of Leading in Schools

ONE FINE BIRD / PRESS
Lawrence, Kansas USA

Arlington, Virginia USA

2111 Wilson Boulevard, Suite 300 · Arlington, VA 22201 USA
Phone: 800-933-2723 or 703-578-9600
Website: www.ascd.org · Email: member@ascd.org
Author guidelines: www.ascd.org/write

Richard Culatta, *Chief Executive Officer*; Anthony Rebora, *Chief Content Officer*; Genny Ostertag, *Managing Director, Book Acquisitions & Editing*; Susan Hills, *Senior Acquisitions Editor*; Mary Beth Nielsen, *Director, Book Editing*; Megan Doyle, *Editor*; Masie Chong, *Senior Graphic Designer*; Valerie Younkin, *Senior Production Designer*; Kelly Marshall, *Production Manager*; Shajuan Martin, *E-Publishing Specialist*; Christopher Logan, *Senior Production Specialist*

ONE FINE BIRD/PRESS
853 N. 1663 Road
Lawrence, KS 66049
Phone: 308-496-4724 · Email: hello@instructionalcoaching.com
Website: www.instructionalcoaching.com

Cover Design by Nadia Standard

Interior Design by Nadia Standard

Copyright © 2026 Instructional Coaching Group. All rights reserved. It is illegal to reproduce copies of this work in print or electronic format (including reproductions displayed on a secure intranet or stored in a retrieval system or other electronic storage device from which copies can be made or displayed) without the prior written permission of the publisher. By purchasing only authorized electronic or print editions and not participating in or encouraging piracy of copyrighted materials, you support the rights of authors and publishers. Readers who wish to reproduce or republish excerpts of this work in print or electronic format may do so for a small fee by contacting the Copyright Clearance Center (CCC), 222 Rosewood Dr., Danvers, MA 01923, USA (phone: 978-750-8400; fax: 978-646-8600; web: www.copyright.com). To inquire about site licensing options or any other reuse, contact ASCD Permissions at www.ascd.org/permissions or permissions@ascd.org. Send translation inquiries to translations@ascd.org.

ASCD® is a registered trademark of Association for Supervision and Curriculum Development. All other trademarks contained in this book are the property of, and reserved by, their respective owners, and are used for editorial and informational purposes only. No such use should be construed to imply sponsorship or endorsement of the book by the respective owners.

All web links in this book are correct as of the publication date below but may have become inactive or otherwise modified since that time. If you notice a deactivated or changed link, please email books@ascd.org with the words "Link Update" in the subject line. In your message, please specify the web link, the book title, and the page number on which the link appears.

PAPERBACK ISBN: 978-1-4166-3414-0   ASCD product #126016   n10/25

PDF E-BOOK ISBN: 978-1-4166-3415-7; see Books in Print for other formats.

Quantity discounts are available: email programteam@ascd.org or call 800-933-2723, ext. 5773, or 703-575-5773. For desk copies, go to www.ascd.org/deskcopy.

Library of Congress Cataloging-in-Publication Data
Names: Munro, Chris, author | Campbell, John (Leadership coach) author
Title: Growth talk : a coaching way of leading in schools / Chris Munro and John Campbell.
Description: Arlington, Virginia : ASCD, [2026] | Includes bibliographical references and index
Identifiers: LCCN 2025026536 (print) | LCCN 2025026537 (ebook) | ISBN 9781416634140 paperback | ISBN 9781416634157 pdf
Subjects: LCSH: Educational leadership | Teachers—In-service training | Employees—Coaching of
    Classification: LCC LB2806 .M824 2025 (print) | LCC LB2806 (ebook)
LC record available at https://lccn.loc.gov/2025026536
LC ebook record available at https://lccn.loc.gov/2025026537

---

35 34 33 32 31 30 29 28 27 26 25   1 2 3 4 5 6 7 8 9 10 11 12

From Chris:
To Monica, who has walked the path as an educator alongside me since our university days and has been a constant source of love, support, and inspiration.

From John:
To Nathan. The world is a better place because of the work that you do.

GROWTH TALK

A Coaching Way of Leading in Schools

Foreword by Jim Knight xi
Preface xv
Acknowledgments xix

PART 1: COACHING AS A WAY OF LEADING

Chapter 1. Conversations: The Currency of School Life 3
Chapter 2. On Being a Conversation Leader 9
Chapter 3. A Continuum of Conversations 18
Chapter 4. The Learning Conversations Map 25

PART 2: THE TOOLS AND TECHNIQUES OF COACHING

Chapter 5. Bringing Shape to Conversations: The GROWTH Framework 41
Chapter 6. Fueling Conversations: Key Skills 53
Chapter 7. Showing Up in Conversations: A Coaching Way of Being 80

PART 3: A COACHING APPROACH IN LESS FORMAL CONTEXTS

Chapter 8. Other-Initiated Conversations: "Got a Minute?" 91
Chapter 9. Leader-Initiated Conversations: "Can We Chat?" 111

PART 4: TAKING A WIDER AND LONGER VIEW

Chapter 10. Everyone a Conversation Leader: Toward a Coaching Culture 131
References 142
Index 147
About the Authors 154

Foreword:
A New Kind of Leadership

When people talk about leadership, they often define it as something like "motivating and inspiring others to commit to a vision and achieve a shared goal." Leaders, according to this definition, are people with excellent communication skills, emotional intelligence, and charisma who get people fired up so that they can join with others to accomplish great things that the leader has identified. This is a great way of defining one approach to leadership. But to my mind, to fully understand leadership, we need a new way to understand what leaders do. Chris Munro and John Campbell help us understand just what this new kind of leadership is. They call it a coaching way of leading.

All of us are leaders. We lead as teachers, principals, colleagues, parents, or community members. Much of what we call life involves leading others, but getting people fired up and moving them toward the same vision probably isn't the primary goal for many of the leadership challenges we face. Often, what we are trying to do as leaders is to create the conditions for others to flourish. We are not trying to control, direct, or motivate others—we are trying, as Sir John Whitmore famously said about coaching, to "unlock... people's potential to maximize their own performance."

As a leader of a B Corp, I know how difficult this kind of leadership can be. We want results now. We see the moral urgency of change happening quickly. And because we have been raised in traditional, hierarchical organizations, we find ourselves relying on the old techniques—trying to motivate, control, or, at worst, micromanage people. But when we control and micromanage, people usually become too reliant on our ideas and guidance, and our directive approach limits people's ability to think for themselves. So, we back off to give people the freedom to be more creative. However, when we give people autonomy, nothing seems to happen. So we go back to micromanaging, and so it goes—we toggle back and forth between control and autonomy.

Chris and John's book gives us the tools to take a new approach to leading—the coaching approach. They teach us how to lead in a way that empowers people so they can make the kinds of choices that are good for the children and adults in our schools. Chris and John describe the theory behind this coaching way of leading, but they also give us practical, useful tools so we can be better as leaders in our schools, communities, and homes.

Growth Talk is, as the title makes clear, a book about conversations that help us grow. This is important because good leaders most certainly must have good conversations. Chris and John help us better understand learning conversations by providing insightful big-picture tools, such as a learning conversations map we can use to figure out the different types of conversations we have—from serious and formal ones to relaxed and casual ones—and use that knowledge to have better learning conversations. At the same time, they provide a wealth of specific practices we can use to put ideas into action. This book offers both a broad view—so we understand formal, informal, leader-led, and partner-led conversations—and, at the same time, describes specific conversational skills: listening, questioning, paraphrasing, and noticing. These are skills that anyone can apply today during learning conversations, and the authors include helpful tips, strategies, and checklists.

To give shape to coaching as a way of leading, the authors describe formal and informal coaching frameworks and processes. John and Chris provide an overview of their GROWTH coaching framework, a proven structure for coaching that they have been studying for decades. I've used the GROWTH coaching framework for close to 10 years, and I know from my experience that it is a powerful, efficient way to partner with others during formal coaching conversations.

At the same time—and this might be the book's most significant contribution—they recognize that coaching often happens in brief conversations. The authors provide guidance on how leaders can help others unlock their hidden abilities in short "got a minute?" conversations. John and Chris explain how to use components of the GROWTH framework, focusing on three key questions: What's wanted? What's working? What's next? They also explain how coaching, whether formal or informal, is brought to life through a way of being that communicates to our conversation partners that we appreciate and believe in their power to think for themselves.

In *Growth Talk*, Chris Munro and John Campbell give us something all of us can use—an approach to leadership that helps us do the challenging, complex, and important work of leading in our lives. Whether we're engaging in formal or informal conversations, this book gives us the tools we need to stop commanding others and start empowering them. This is a book about a new kind of leadership, grounded in partnership, caring, and unlocking potential. I also think this is exactly the book we need right now to lead our schools, our students, our communities, and our families.

—**Jim Knight**, founding senior partner of the Instructional Coaching Group (ICG)

Preface

In the spirit of the work we are about introduce, we chose to open this book with a question: What did you learn on the job today?

If you are drawing a blank in response to this question, perhaps you need to dig deeper by reflecting on the conversations you participated in today. Every conversation we have holds the promise of deeper learning; however, not every conversation delivers on this promise. In the pages that follow, you will learn how to maximize the conversations you have as a way to promote learning and generate progress.

CONVERSATION IS AT THE HEART OF LEARNING AND LEADING

Our premise is that the best Growth Talk conversations are those that bring the key elements of coaching into play. Coaching and education share common goals. Both aspire to support learning, growth, and development. Yet, in most schools, coaching is framed as a unique and formal type of engagement that is separate from our normal, day-to-day interactions such as those we have with our students in classrooms, meetings with other staff members, or the impromptu hallway conversations that take place every working day. We believe that the principles and practices of coaching (e.g., ability to listen to others, ask questions, summarize, and notice) have far broader applicability than solely formal arrangements, and our aim, therefore, is to broaden your perspective on the uses of coaching.

While nearly all of us engage in talking, our focus here is on *how* we talk and *what* we talk about. Just as words have the power to help or harm us, talk can enable or inhibit positive change. This book is about how to intentionally utilize the key skills, techniques, and dispositions that have such a powerful impact in formal coaching situations in other, less formal conversational contexts.

We also believe that "coaching as way of leading" isn't a euphemism for manipulating our staff into helping us realize our (and our school's) goals. We go so far as to suggest that this form of leadership can restore educator trust, well-being, and hope at a time when many education professionals feel under-appreciated and depleted. In doing so, it also has a positive impact on our students' well-being and overall success in schools and beyond. Coaching is, above all, a human endeavor that, in the best instances, serves to elevate human potential. As such, coaching as a way of leading has the potential to bring renewed focus to the humanity of our schools and systems by bringing us closer to becoming the best versions of ourselves.

COACHING AS A WAY OF LEADING

In this book, we use *coaching as a way of leading* to describe a people-centered form of leadership that enhances relational trust and wellbeing through more agency-enabling conversations that support learning, growth, and progress. While those in formal educational leadership positions are a natural audience for this book, our premise is that anyone can be a conversation leader, regardless of their job title or role. We can all learn to engage in humanizing conversations that foster more trusting relationships and support purposeful dialogue. In doing so, we can have a more positive impact on the success and well-being of our students, staff, and their communities.

When we think of schools as living, dynamic networks of people communicating with one another to pursue common goals, it follows that we want to focus on improving our conversations. Moreover, since the primary mission of schools is to promote learning and growth, it stands to reason that our conversations should also further this mission.

WHO SHOULD READ THIS BOOK?

Although we wrote this book primarily for K–12 education professionals, the principles of *Growth Talk* also apply to many other professions. But schools are unique in that they aspire to promote learning and growth for both children and adults. Therefore, we encourage our readers to consider every interaction between members of a school community as a potential opportunity to enhance learning, growth, and progress—a potential that can be brought to life through applying the skills of what we call *learning conversations*. All teachers, administrators, specialists, and school support staff stand to benefit by learning and mastering these skills.

A BRIEF WALKTHROUGH OF THE BOOK

Full disclosure: If you are in search of a comprehensive guide to formal coaching principles and practices, this is *not* the book for you. Rather, we have attempted to distill the essence of effective coaching into a brief guide for those who wish to apply the growth-enhancing elements of coaching to the conversations they have in a variety of contexts—from formal interactions to those impromptu encounters that can become "coachable moments." Following is an overview of the chapters. Figure P.1 provides a graphic overview.

PART 1: COACHING AS A WAY OF LEADING

Chapters 1–4 lay out the case for coaching as a way of leading and present research and frameworks for making sense of the conversations that support the thinking, learning, and progress of others.

PART 2: THE TOOLS AND TECHNIQUES OF COACHING

Chapters 5–7 introduce the key skills, techniques, and dispositions that help leaders lead and manage conversations.

PART 3: A COACHING APPROACH IN LESS FORMAL CONTEXTS

Chapters 8 and 9 illustrate how to apply the key skills, techniques, and dispositions of coaching in less formal conversational contexts. Key topics include offering effective feedback and building agility as a conversation leader, especially in those impromptu conversations we have no time to prepare for. These less formal conversations are the lifeblood of leadership and can be either other-initiated or leader-initiated. In either case, they present the opportunity to be learning conversations when skillfully and intentionally managed by the conversation leader.

PART 4: TAKING A WIDER AND LONGER VIEW

Chapter 10 asks readers to consider how these brief conversations can have a big impact over time and when this kind of discourse becomes more widespread across the organization. We pose the question "What if everyone was a more effective conversation leader?" and explore what this might mean in terms of creating a coaching culture for learning.

FIGURE P.1
Growth Talk Flow Chart

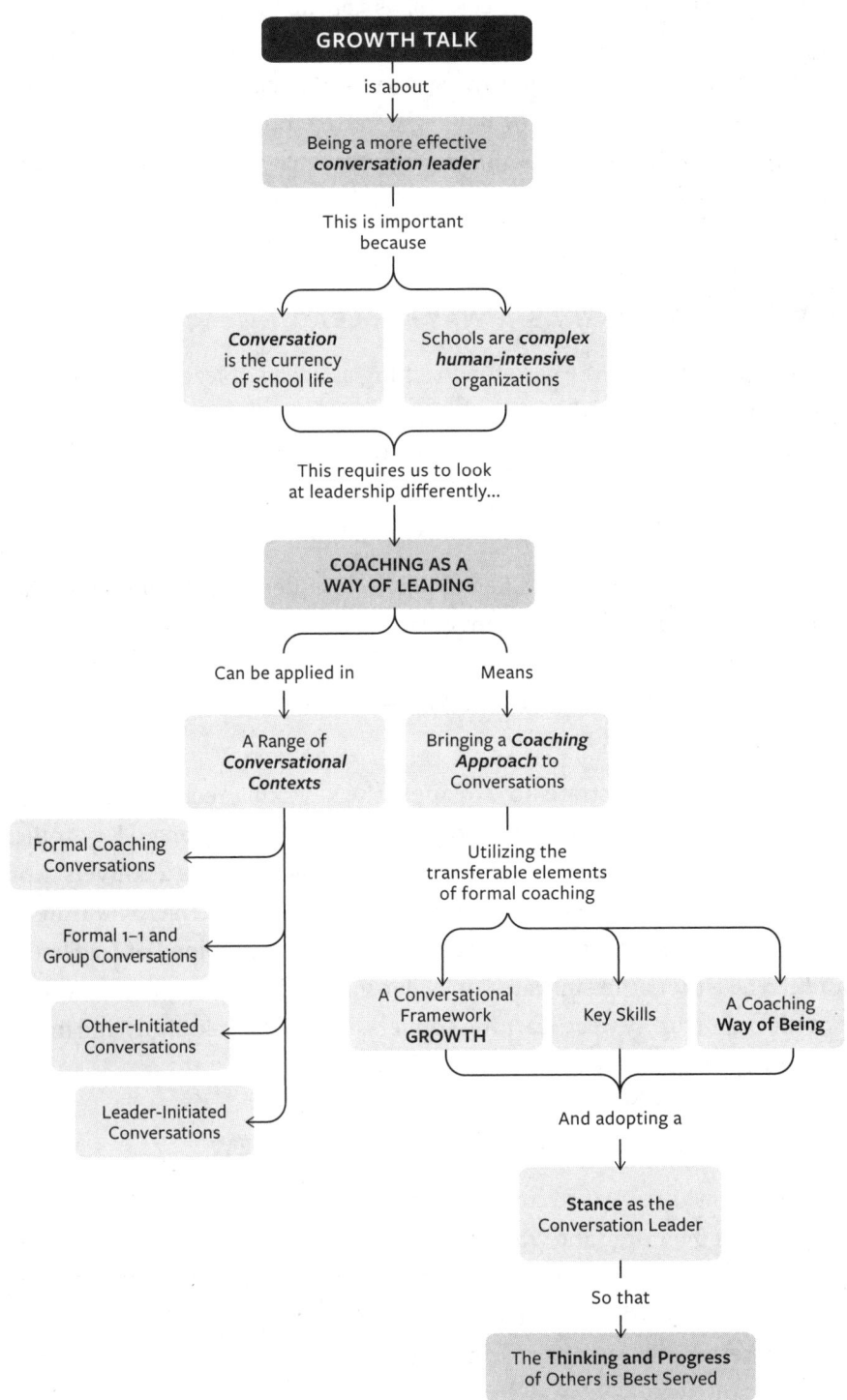

Acknowledgments

This book has been a long time in gestation, and we are grateful for the support and insights we have gained from colleagues, friends, and clients.

Growth Talk would not exist without the initial conversations John had with Dr. Christian van Nieuwerburgh while driving around the English countryside almost a decade ago. Further discussions with our former colleague Jason Pascoe and work by the late Professor Tony Grant were also influential in refining and advancing our thinking. Our friend and colleague Dr. Jim Knight was a constant encourager. He nudged and urged us to complete this project when we were sometimes distracted by pressing matters in our day jobs.

In the end, we think that the finished product has benefited from an extended period of drafting, discussing, testing and refining. Our wonderful colleagues at Growth Coaching International and the Instructional Coaching Group have, like us, been immersed in the work of supporting school leaders and their education communities for many years, and they have undoubtedly shaped the thinking and ideas in our book. We are especially thankful for our many learning conversations with Claudia Owad, Debbie Lowe, Dan Steele, Mary Webb, Penny Verdich, Gray Ryan, Di Henning, and Nicky Knight.

Over the past couple of years, we have presented and trialled the key frameworks and concepts of *Growth Talk* with some of our trusted clients. We are especially grateful for the support of the New South Wales School Leadership Institute and the Victorian Academy of Teaching and Leadership, who engaged with some of this material as part of their leadership development programs.

In addition to the wisdom of two prolific authors and experts in our field in Christian van Nieuwerburgh and Jim Knight, we have benefitted from the support of some of the most experienced and talented editors in the business. Dan Alpert provided expert guidance and encouragement as we wrestled with expressing and organizing our ideas. He added enormous value to the final product. Kirsten McBride brought another keen set of editorial eyes to the text and helped refine our language and figures even further. We are also thankful for the excellent design work that Nadia Standard has contributed to this book. The cover design, figures, and internal layout elevate our humble manuscript to something that we hope readers will enjoy engaging with. We are also grateful to our colleagues at One Fine Bird Press and ASCD who brought considerable expertise, patience, and good humor to the management of the publication process, especially Jenny Knight, Megan Doyle, and Susan Hills.

Last but certainly not least, we acknowledge the support of our families who have graciously shared their lives (and homes) with our work for many years.

We continue to be inspired by the work of our colleagues in the field of coaching in education and by the countless educators around the globe who have engaged with our work. Many of them have become friends as a result of our shared passion for enhancing the quality of conversations in education communities.

01

Coaching as a Way of Leading

Chapter 1. Conversations: The Currency of School Life

Chapter 2. On Being a Conversation Leader

Chapter 3. A Continuum of Conversations

Chapter 4. The Learning Conversations Map

CHAPTER 1

Conversations: The Currency of School Life

> *"We live in worlds our conversations create."*
> DAVID COOPERRIDER (2018)

In a world where complexity and ambiguity define our everyday existence, one truth holds firm: We need each other. Humans are, by nature, social creatures. We depend upon one another to meet a wide range of needs, beginning with our very survival as infants and across our lifespans. In addition, we learn from others, typically beginning with parents or other adults in our lives and later from peers, teachers, and others with knowledge to share—whether in the form of lessons, professional development, meetings, or informal gatherings.

Learning can happen in conversations, but not all conversations are what we call *learning conversations*. Some conversations are necessarily transactional in nature. Consider the following telephone exchange:

"Hello. I'd like to place a delivery order for two large pizzas, one with pepperoni and one with mushrooms."

"Sir, what is your telephone number?"

"(Responds with telephone number.)"

"I see you are in our system. Is your address still 6200 Pleasant View Road in Pleasantview?"

"Yes."

"OK. Just to confirm: You want two large, one mushroom and one pepperoni, right?"

"Yes."

"Cheese on both?"

"Yes."

"OK. Delivery time will be approximately 45 minutes. Use the credit card on file ending in 7239?"

"Yes."

"Anything else?"

"No, thanks."

"Thank you."

Take a moment to reflect on this exchange. Aside from the fact that it isn't particularly interesting, would you say that either party learned *anything* from it? One might argue that that the person who answered the phone learned that the person placing the call resides at the same address as the last time an order was placed. Or, perhaps the knowledge that the restaurant has a system that captures names, addresses, telephone numbers, and credit card data is new information to the caller, but would you still call this transaction a learning conversation? In all likelihood, the answer is "no." And it certainly wasn't growth-producing for either participant.

Unlike this exchange, true learning conversations carry opportunities for personal and professional growth. Such conversations are commonplace in our schools, but unless we deliberately take the time to reflect on them, we may not even recognize that we (or our conversation partners) have learned from them. Consider this extended reflection by a school principal ending their day.

> *It had been a long day! Recently, I started a routine of taking some time to reflect on the day as soon as I got home. It usually takes less than 15 minutes. It has been a revelation! I chose to do this for several reasons. I wanted to gain insights by taking time to reflect. At the same time, I was hoping to remind myself of all the good things that I had managed to do. It turns out that this practice also helps me to "put a lid" on the day and allow myself some time to wind down.*
>
> *The day began well enough. We started with a very productive, high-energy meeting about the new co-teaching project. This was immediately followed by a challenging parent meeting that I had been dreading. Then there was that complaint about the process for appointing new student*

leaders. I knew that Jane would want to make an appointment to talk about that. I got through an awkward meeting with her, and we managed to get to a reasonable resolution.

Later in the morning, I visited a classroom—this is something I try very hard to keep in my schedule. Almost always, these visits are highlights of my day! It is easy to lose sight of the wonderful learning that is taking place in our school every day. With all the crazy demands and unexpected crises, I never want to lose my connection to what really matters. I had some wonderful conversations with students today. They reminded me of why I do what I do!

Before lunch, Irfan stopped me in the corridor to share some progress made on the professional learning day he was leading. It was a short conversation because we were both on our way to separate meetings. But somehow, despite the time pressure, it ended up being a "spirit lifter" for both of us! We both had important "aha" moments during the brief interaction. I look forward to hearing how the plans we discussed progress in the next few weeks. After spending a quiet 15 minutes dealing with emails at my desk, I grabbed some lunch and met up with one of our new teachers and asked how their morning had been. Their response of "Oh, not bad, thanks" carried an underlying anxiety beneath the words, and I got the impression that "not bad" didn't mean good. With students all around, this was not the time to inquire further, however. I wonder if I made them uneasy or if something else was going on? We're all a bit frazzled at the end of semester, never mind being new to our school. I made a mental note to have an informal chat with their mentor.

After lunch, I had my regular coaching session with Ranjit, one of the other principals in our local network. Though I always tell myself that I don't have time to do this, I always find it an extremely satisfying process. It seems that I take away almost as much from each session as Ranjit. I feel like I'm contributing to my own professional growth but also to the growth of our profession.

Finally, the day ended with a Zoom meeting with one of the assistant superintendents to review staffing processes in light of anticipated budget cuts. This was a difficult conversation, and we were both tired, but it was important nonetheless. It had to happen, and I now have a better understanding of what to expect and can begin planning accordingly.

It had been a busy day, and even though I left the building exhausted, upon reflection, it was mostly energizing and positive. Not every workday ends like this. These were the main events that came to mind, but there had been many, many other brief interactions. A couple of those helped to move minor tasks along; others were pleasant but of no real consequence. Most of my days follow a similar pattern, with a collection of scheduled and spontaneous interactions filling up the time. It has been said, "Your life is the summary of how you show up in the interactions you encounter every day!" That seems a pretty good description of how things are unfolding at the moment! I spend most of my day talking with other people. It is exhausting work though, and I've been feeling tired for weeks. Right now, after reflecting on today, I realize that I need to take some time for myself so I can get up and do it all again tomorrow!

This brief reflection captures how a typical day unfolds for many school leaders. Various conversations, planned and unplanned, dominate the day's activities. For the most part, education takes place through relationships and conversations. All educators, including principals, can benefit from the habit of self-reflection, as suggested above. The Putting It into Practice section at the end of this chapter offers some prompts that will help you become more aware of the intents and contexts of your conversations.

Upon reflection, we (John and Chris) are in conversation during much of our workdays in our roles as managers, leaders, facilitators, and coaches. When we look back and reflect on our times as educators and curriculum consultants, we realize that even more talking was going on. Some of these conversations are between the two of us, but most happen with others as we present concepts, seek different perspectives, modify and progress our thoughts, and turn them into actions. And, of course, all that happens in reverse as we listen to the challenges and opportunities others bring to these conversations. Our conversations are quite varied: some are messy, some awkward, and some accelerate progress while others seem to frustrate it. Some conversations are exhilarating, and some can even be life-changing.

How we talk to one another and the quality of our conversations are important drivers of student, educator, and school success. We can construct the most ambitious and brilliant school improvement plans on paper, but we must recognize that conversations are at the heart of every effort to improve the quality of teaching, learning, and everything else that happens within school communities and, therefore, deserve particular attention. Judith Glaser, an expert on organizational communication, sums up this idea as follows:

> *To get to the next level of greatness depends on the quality of our culture, which depends on the quality of our relationships, which depends on the quality of our conversations. Everything happens through conversations. (Glaser, 2014, p. 34)*

We also believe that the impact of our conversations can extend far beyond our core mission of teaching and learning by helping to restore humanity to a profession that continues to be subjected to a deficit-focused, dehumanizing narrative of teacher underperformance and mediocrity. As for any profession (or just about any human endeavor, for that matter), we acknowledge that there is always room for improvement. However, at the same time, we must not lose sight of all the small miracles that are enacted in classrooms and schools every day. Now, more than ever before, the challenges faced by K–12 professionals and their students can be overwhelming. School principals and classroom teachers continue to exit the profession in droves. The toll of the COVID-19 pandemic keeps surfacing in the form of growing mental health challenges for both educators and the students they serve.

It is time to change the narrative to one that is strengths-based and in which teachers are treated as thinking professionals who can be trusted to do the complex and demanding work of teaching and learning. And, unlike the exchange around ordering a pizza, our conversations can and do change lives. We (your authors) believe that shifting our schools and education systems from enterprises that are transactional to those that are transformational begins with shifting the nature of our conversations so they promote learning and growth every day.

It may sound lofty, but we believe that when educators improve the quality of conversations in school communities, they can open possibilities that were never before envisioned for themselves and, more importantly, for their students. The following chapters offer frameworks, principles, and practical approaches to help the conversations that you lead stimulate thinking, growth, and progress for others.

PUTTING IT INTO PRACTICE

REFLECTING ON YOUR CONVERSATION CONTEXTS

Imagine going back to your diary or calendar for the past month or term and making note of all the conversations that were not entered as appointments or meetings. Then reflect on the following:

- Who were the conversations with (e.g., students, parents, team members, leadership team members)?
- What were the topics or functions of these conversations? And what were the contexts or settings—more formal or less formal?
- What were the outcomes of the conversations?
- How might you have revised one of these conversations in a manner that would have helped your conversation partner learn and grow?

CHAPTER 2

ON BEING A CONVERSATION LEADER

> *"One great conversation can shift the direction of change forever."*
> LINDA LAMBERT (1995)

SCHOOLS AS HUMAN-INTENSIVE SYSTEMS

Recent research in complexity and systems theory has challenged traditional industrial-age views of organizations. The old metaphors that likened organizations to factory assembly lines failed to consider the complexity of human behavior. Such metaphors are especially problematic when applied to organizations like schools. Any of us who has devoted endless hours to constructing strategic plans in pursuit of ambitious outcomes has experienced the disappointing realization that humans, unlike widgets and robots, are a unique resource that demands a far more sophisticated approach to management. Given this complexity, it should come as no surprise that machine and factory metaphors have been replaced by those that highlight the social connections and relationships at the heart of how work gets done.

Today's organizational scholars often use language like "complex adaptive systems;" however, we prefer the term *human-intensive systems* when considering educational contexts like schools. Researchers have highlighted how these kinds of human systems are characterized by active agents—people—who choose, learn, and communicate with other agents within the system in non-linear and unpredictable ways (McDaniel, 2007). We now understand the way in which organizations, particularly knowledge-based organizations, consist of fluid, interconnected networks of people talking to each other to achieve common goals. It follows that schools could be characterized as quintessential human-intensive systems, since the learning within them depends largely on the nature and quality of conversations.

SCHOOLS AS SOCIAL NETWORKS

The study of social networks provides another helpful lens on the role of conversation within organizations. Two studies in particular have made an important contribution to our understanding of the internal workings of organizational life and how collaboration, organizational energy, innovation, and productivity are generated and sustained.

In *The Hidden Power of Social Networks* (2004), researchers Rob Cross and Andrew Parker drew particular attention to how organizational energy fuels success as well as how the lack of this energy sabotages success. Their research uncovered some valuable patterns in the relationships that generate positive energy. The five components of Cross and Parker's positive energy interactions are the following (Cross & Parker, 2004, 57–63, emphasis added):

- **A compelling goal:** a focus on what *could be* rather than on what *is* or *has been*.
- **A meaningful contribution:** a focus that allows others to feel they are heard and can make a contribution and can influence the interaction.
- **A sense of engagement:** a focus on being fully present both psychologically and physically.
- **The perception of progress:** a focus on movement and "getting somewhere."
- **The belief that the idea being discussed can succeed:** a sense that the topic of the interaction is worthwhile and can be attained.

When these components were present, Cross and Parker noted that the conversations were more likely to achieve useful outcomes, where ideas progressed and relationships were enhanced.

In another study, Jane Dutton (2003) described how high-quality connections developed when respectful engagement and task-enabling practices were present.

- *Respectful engagement* involves engaging others in ways that communicate value and worth. Dutton outlines five key features for this: "being present, being genuine, communicating affirmation, effective listening, supportive communication" (pp. 21–52).
- *Task enabling* involves interacting with others to facilitate another person's successful performance.

Both studies describe skills and practices that closely resemble those we have used in our coaching work with educators for more than 20 years. These researchers were not coaches, nor were they researching coaching or setting out to identify coaching practices. Yet, they discovered that certain individuals—Cross and Parker's "positive energizers"—exhibited coach-like practices in their personal interactions, including the following:

- Building a foundation of trust.
- Establishing and sustaining a goal or outcome focus.
- Being present for and authentically listening to others.
- Affirming others' strengths.
- Making and affirming progress toward desired outcomes.

Not only would most of these practices appear on any list of what effective coaches do, but we believe that a "coaching way of leading" might just be the best-fit leadership style in contemporary education settings. Moreover, the use of such practices shouldn't be limited to those in formal administrative or supervisory positions. A coaching approach to conversations among all members of the community has the potential to enhance levels of understanding, collaboration, and learning across the whole organization.

While the two studies above focused primarily on the corporate sector, we believe that, in human-intensive organizations like schools, conversations play an even greater role. Interactions between school leaders and teachers, teachers and teachers, teachers and administrators, and teachers and parents are an essential component of school life. Perhaps even more important, in a school, the learning conversations between teachers and students are at the heart of what a school is all about.

LEADING THROUGH CONVERSATIONS IN HUMAN-INTENSIVE SYSTEMS

Our work at GCI has led us to think a lot about leading and what people do when leading well. The research and literature on leading continue to evolve, as do our organizations and the world at large. The literature is replete with theories and research findings about the nature of leadership. Traditional leadership theories tend to focus on who or what the leader is or *does* and locate leadership within an individual. As such, they focus on traits, character, and skills that leaders bring to their work. While some of this work offers helpful insights, for us, the practice of effective leadership is grounded in high levels of conversational and relationship-building skills. Systems-based approaches focus on a leader's relationship with their followers (Groysberg & Slind, 2012; Walker & Aritz, 2014) and propose that leadership emerges through the interactions of people—when interactions create change, growth, and movement, positive things happen.

Before we talk about leading through conversations, we need to define further what we mean by leadership in human-intensive organizations. We are influenced by the work of Peter Northouse (2024), who suggests that "leadership is a process where an individual influences a group of individuals to achieve a common goal" (p. 2). We are attracted to the simplicity of this statement, yet every word has richness and subtlety. Our adapted version of Northouse's definition takes a similar shape but makes some significant modifications:

> *Leadership is a process where an individual facilitates the movement of other individuals and teams towards new things—aligned goals, attitudes, capabilities and skills—that currently do not exist in the ways that people would like them to. The fundamental way a leader accomplishes this movement (or progress) is through skilfully led, purposeful conversations.*

Like Northouse, we believe that leadership is a process driven by particular types of interactions between leaders and followers. And like Northouse, we emphasize movement or progress, since all leadership is about helping people move from one point to another. This is especially so when responding to the complexities of leading effective teaching and learning, whether supporting student learning and agency or helping our colleagues progress toward individual and/or organizational goals. Further, the intentional conversations that we have with individuals and groups drive such progress.

Since conversations are a nearly universal aspect of the human experience, it is not a stretch to suggest that any of us (including those without formal leadership positions or titles) can take the lead in these conversations.

One's capacity to lead through conversations requires equal parts awareness, skill, and flexibility—the very ideas we will explore more fully in the coming pages.

KEY FEATURES OF LEADING THROUGH CONVERSATIONS

Evidence from research and practice supports a shift toward conversational approaches as critical components of leadership (Glaser, 2014; Hurley & Brown, 2010). Some common features have emerged from this body of work: sensemaking, learning, experimentation, and progress.

SENSEMAKING

In our extension of Northouse's definition, conversation leaders help us to (a) make sense of new, ambiguous, or confusing circumstances; (b) bring clarity to others; and (c) initiate steps that lead to movement and progress. Organizational scholars have identified sensemaking as an important leadership practice (Ancona, 2012; McDaniel, 2007). *Sensemaking* is typically defined as helping people make meaning and sense from disparate, fragmented, and new experiences. Reuben McDaniel (2007), a scholar and expert on complexity theory, extended this and defined sensemaking as "turning circumstances into a situation that is comprehended explicitly in words and serves as a springboard to action" (p. 28).

Amid rapid change and shifting foundations, we often struggle to gain some sense of meaning and clarity and to figure out what's going on. McDaniel elaborated on sensemaking as follows: "We want workers to make sense of their worlds in ways that *enhance, rather than inhibit,* the organization's ability to take effective action and to learn from that action" (our emphasis in italics; McDaniel, 2007, p. 30).

Sensemaking captures the essence of what happens in a coaching conversation: A coach or conversation leader listens, asks questions, and uses language to support their coachee toward gaining clarity and insight. In many ways, educators do something similar every day; they help people enact a change—learning and applying new content, mastering a new task, and so on—through the words they use. Educators can create better environments for learning, development, and growth within their organizational settings by stepping up to lead conversations.

SENSEMAKING QUESTIONS

In many ways, all coaching conversations serve a "sensemaking" purpose. Specific questions that can prompt sensemaking include the following:

- **What's most on your mind about this matter?** This question, following a brief background statement about what might be of concern, is often enough to stimulate cut-through thinking to help prioritize the various components of the concern and bring greater clarity.
- **What are the three most important pieces of this topic for you right now?** Questions that help others focus on right-now immediacy are often helpful sensemaking questions.
- **What would be of most concern to others about this topic?** Questions that prompt a change of perspective can often help to broaden awareness and bring greater clarity.

LEARNING

Readers who taught in or led schools during the COVID-19 pandemic will attest to the fact that in an environment of rapid change and unpredictability, we can no longer depend on business as usual. When faced with novel circumstances, our ability to adapt depends upon new learning, as teachers experienced when they had to learn to maximize online teaching and learning during the pandemic. According to McDaniel (2007), "People don't know what to do not because they are incompetent but because they have not seen the present situation before. They must constantly figure it out" (p. 21). We can facilitate the process of "figuring things out" by engaging in learning conversations.

Learning needs to be constant and ongoing to spark innovation and progress. In their seminal text *Professional Capital*, Hargreaves and Fullan (2012) draw our attention to the need for "next practices" (in addition to well-founded best practices) to emerge in schools. These next practices don't necessarily come from the top down; instead, "innovative approaches… often begin with teachers themselves, and that will sometimes turn out to be the best practices of the future" (Hargreaves & Fullan, 2012, p. 51). The leader's task, then, is to enable an environment where learning is highly valued. One way to do this is to be a "multiplier" (Wiseman, 2017), a leader whose response to complexity and challenge is to think, "There are smart people everywhere who will figure this out and get even smarter in the process," and who sees their job as bringing the right people together in an environment that liberates everyone's best thinking.

LEARNING QUESTIONS

Learning is central to any coaching conversation. Specific questions that can prompt learning include the following:

- **What successes have you had in the past in similar situations?** Prompting a focus on the resourceful past can stimulate useful learning.
- **Who do you know who handles these situations well? What might they do?** Prompting a focus on resourceful people around them can stimulate useful learning.

EXPERIMENTATION

Experimentation, in the context of learning conversations, is an iterative process based on small actions: feedback, learning, and adaptation. Try something; if it works, do more of it; if it doesn't work, try something else. Learn from both success and failure and adapt quickly. In this way, a virtuous cycle of inquiry is enacted that increases the odds of success. We emphasize "adapt quickly" because, as we learned during the pandemic, in environments characterized by rapid change and unpredictability, agility and flexibility are often far more valuable than the best-laid strategic plans.

Learning conversations support cultures of experimentation. That is, conversation leaders support others to envision a desired state or outcome, formulate indicators of progress toward this outcome, and take action. Experimentation implies the freedom to make choices; however, even the most creative endeavors are subject to constraints such as rules. Think about the structure of poetry as an example. A haiku poet has the freedom to choose words, subjects, and imagery; however, they must do so within a three-line form with a prescribed syllabic structure. Similarly, in schools, the "form" within which experimentation takes place may be influenced by a vision or mission, a strategic plan, agreed policies and practices, and guiding models and frameworks.

EXPERIMENTATION QUESTIONS

When we inject any change, however small, into a situation, we impact the situation in some way. Doing something changes things. Doing nothing hardly ever does. Some questions that can prompt experimentation include the following:

- What might be a small change you could make that would move this topic forward? What would you learn from this if you did it?
- What might be a low risk/high learning action that would generate insights about the situation and the people involved?

PROGRESS

As noted earlier, our definition of leadership emphasizes progress, or moving things forward. Conversation leaders who support others in making progress through the actions they take possess a critical skill. Amabile and Kramer (2011) identified enabling even small-step progress as one of the most important things leaders could do to help generate engagement and positive energy. And as we noted earlier, Cross and Parker (2004) identified a perception of progress as one of the most important positive energizers emerging from leaders' interactions with colleagues. Talk is good, but talk is best when it leads to something happening. When something happens, it changes the game, even in small ways. Positive actions, even tiny ones, always help move things forward.

PROGRESS QUESTIONS

A sense of progress does not need to be large to create positive energy and momentum. Some questions that can prompt progress include the following:

- **So, where is your thinking up to on this now?** This type of question calls upon us to summarize the current state of our thinking and, in the process, focus on what we need to do to progress or deepen it.
- **What might be a tiny step you could take to move this forward? When will you do it?** These questions move from exploration to action, creating movement. Adding a specific reference to when things might happen helps lock it in. Writing it down, when appropriate, consolidates it even further.

These four features—sensemaking, learning, experimentation, and progress—are highly desirable outcomes of well-led conversations in human-intensive learning organizations like schools. The good news is that, with appropriate training and opportunities for practice, anyone can take the lead in everyday conversations. More specifically, when we develop and hone the conversational skills in our repertoire, we become conscious of how we "show up" for others in our interactions. The guiding principle of this book is that a coaching way of leading energizes the entire school community in a manner that honors our collective humanity, enhances our well-being, fuels our learning, and supports our progress toward attaining the most ambitious of goals.

As psychologist and author Harlene Anderson puts it:

> *We are in continuous conversation with each other and with ourselves. Through conversations we form and reform our life experiences and events; we create and recreate our meanings and understandings; and we construct our realities and ourselves. Some conversations enhance possibility; others diminish it. (Kelm, 2005, p. 10).*

The ways in which we might shape our way of conversing so that we enhance possibility rather than diminish it are at the core of this work.

PUTTING IT INTO PRACTICE

Take a moment to reflect on how the theory and concepts presented in this chapter relate to your experience of leadership, learning, and change. The following prompts might help you:

- In your experience, is leadership of a school and all that it entails, more like overseeing a well-oiled machine—predictable, mechanical, aligned, consistent, complicated—or like kayaking down an unfamiliar river—less predictable, smooth patches and rough patches, requiring navigation and course correction, dynamic, complex?
- What are some examples from your own practice that fit each of these metaphors?
- How do the key features of leading through conversations in human-intensive organizations—sensemaking, learning, experimentation, and progress—relate to your leadership contexts and conversations?

CHAPTER 3

A Continuum of Conversations

> *"If either the quality of the performance or learning from the experience is important, coaching is a must. If neither is, then tell—if you must."*
> **JOHN WHITMORE (2009)**

Our colleague, instructional coaching expert Jim Knight, has written that "our schools are only as good as the conversations within them" (Knight, 2016, p. 4). Powerful conversations are especially important in educational organizations because communication is at the heart of everything educators do. The good news is that we can learn to lead positive conversations. In his bestselling book, *Better Conversations* (2016), Knight describes how we can get better at the kind of conversations that help us be better communicators and people. This book takes the position that the most powerful conversations are learning conversations—the subject matter of this chapter.

We define learning conversations as interactions that provide opportunities to intentionally seek, support, or amplify learning. In school settings, these frequently include conversations about learning. In a learning conversation, the conversation leader consciously acts in service of their partner's thinking and progress. These often spontaneous conversations promote learning that could include new insights and understanding, greater clarity, and increased awareness, all of which increase our motivation and commitment to make progress.

Through our professional learning work with coaches, mentors, and educational leaders, we have deepened our understanding of how to promote and normalize more intentional conversations that support learning. The continuum of conversations depicted in Figure 3.1 is an especially useful concept that has emerged from our work with educators (Munro, 2020, 2022; Munro & Campbell, 2022).

FIGURE 3.1
A Continuum of Conversations in Education Settings

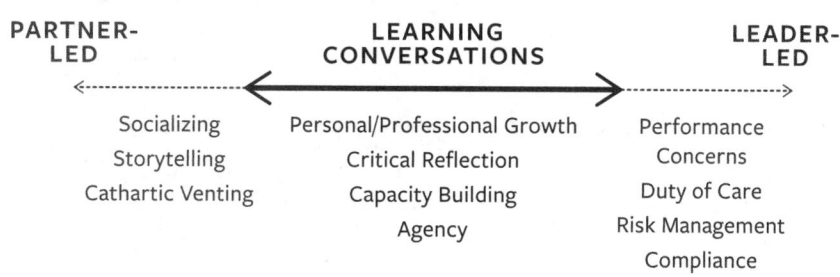

As illustrated, partner-led conversations appear on the left-hand side of the continuum; at the opposite end are leader-led conversations. The terms "leader-led" and "partner-led" refer to the degree to which the conversation leader initiates the interaction, manages it, and provides direction and advice, or not. In other words, they refer to the degree to which the conversation leader's voice and agenda feature in the conversation.

You have no doubt experienced times when you, or perhaps somebody on your staff or a peer, just wanted to be heard; maybe a teacher wanted to air their frustrations about the lack of time to complete everything they set out to accomplish. In such situations, an unstructured, agenda-free social interaction—that is, an entirely partner-led conversation—is appropriate. At the other end of the continuum, the leader-led end, think about situations that require your direction. For example, setting a firm agenda, communicating an unambiguous imperative, or signaling a clear call to action.

What's important here is that conversations that begin at either end of the continuum can develop into learning opportunities. Such conversations may raise the awareness of our conversation partner to the point where they become what Paul Jackson and Mark McKergow (2007) call "a customer for change"—someone who, as a result of the conversation, now sees a compelling need for something to change *and* wants to do something about it. This leaves a significant proportion of the continuum where our conversation partner is already a customer for change and the opportunity for learning presents itself immediately.

A CONVERSATION LEADER

Throughout this book we use the terms *conversation leader* and *conversation partner* to denote the person leading or managing the conversation and the person being supported respectively. Our proposition is that the continuum of learning conversations represents a wide range of interactions that have the potential for anyone, formally or otherwise, to support the learning of another.

THREE STANCES OF A CONVERSATION LEADER

Over time, effective conversation leaders develop the ability to support learning conversations through an understanding and application of stance.

Dictionary definitions of the word *stance* offer two meanings, both of which can be applied to conversations. The first, a way of standing or our posture, could mean how we literally position ourselves during the conversation. The more figurative meaning of the word is less about physical positioning and more about an intellectual or emotional orientation.

Think about how you position yourself in a conversation depending on the needs and capacities of your conversation partner. Ask yourself: Does the conversation need more of me or less of me right now? How can I best support their thinking and help them make progress? Do they have the resources they need to move forward? What's needed from me to help them get there? When leading learning conversations, stance is a combination of how we consciously "show up" and what we do to support the thinking and progress of our conversation partner.

Figure 3.2 describes three distinct stances of a conversation leader. The facilitative and dialogical stances are "partnering" conversations in which the conversation leader positions their partner as the key decision maker (i.e., they have choice about what they want to change and how they will get there). By contrast, the directive stance can be thought of as a "telling" approach. Here, the conversation leader has decided what needs to change and is seeking compliance from their conversation partner. When we adopt a directive stance, we limit choice for our conversation partner (about what must change). The facilitative and dialogical stances are those associated with forms of coaching, whereas a directive stance is not normally associated with coaching.

Notwithstanding these distinctions, all three stances are the domain of educational leaders, and all will feature at some point in leadership conversations. A key premise of this book is that there are far more opportunities and need for partnering conversations than for telling conversations as a leader and, crucially, these conversations best support the learning of those around us. Moreover, highly effective leaders know when to change stance in response to what they are noticing in their conversation partner.

FIGURE 3.2
Three Stances of a Conversation Leader

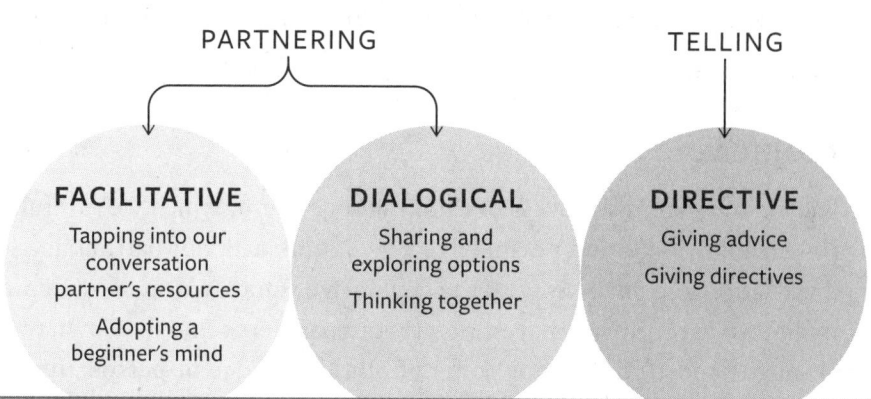

FACILITATIVE

A facilitative stance is an inquiry-based stance designed to tap into our partner's resources. This requires us to adopt a "beginner's mind" and consciously set aside our own knowledge, expertise, and experience to focus on supporting our partner in exploring their own ideas. In this situation, the conversation leader is starting with the view that there is a high likelihood that their partner has the resources (internal and external) to make progress and might already be thinking about the way forward. The leader's primary role in this stance, therefore, is to utilize coaching skills and techniques to facilitate the thinking and progress of their partner.

FACILITATIVE STANCE TIPS

- Notice as they talk. What are you listening *for*? What's wanted instead? What strengths do you hear? Resources? Emotions?

- Pay attention to what you are listening *with*. Curiosity? Respect? Humility? Empathy?
- Use expanders like "And what else?" and "Tell me more about…" to amplify what's wanted.
- Help find resources and options with questions like "What's working now?" "Who else do you know who does this well?" and "Tell me about a time in the past when you have been successful at this or something similar."
- Use paraphrasing to reframe the current reality in terms of what's wanted in the future.
- Summarize and organize what they are verbalising to create momentum.
- Hold the silence when it occurs—it signifies thinking!

DIALOGICAL

A dialogical stance is a process of thinking together in which we carefully share our knowledge and perspective as we think *with* our partner about their situation and goals. As with the facilitative stance, we must maintain an open-minded curiosity that empowers our partner to find their own way while also respectfully sharing some of our knowledge or perspective in support of their thinking and progress. In this situation, the conversation leader notices that their partner has *some* resources but may be having trouble seeing other options or a clear way forward. If the conversation leader has some of the knowledge needed, they share this dialogically—that is, in a way that maintains choice for their partner.

DIALOGICAL STANCE TIPS

- Dialogical does not mean 50-50 turn taking. Our conversation partner should still be doing most of the talking and thinking—aim for at least 70-30.
- Share your knowledge provisionally—you are simply adding options to the pool of available ways forward.
- Always ask permission (e.g., "May I offer some suggestions?").
- Resist the temptation to "sell" your best idea—maintain genuine choice.
- Raise awareness by noticing and reflecting back key terms, patterns, or emotions.

- Avoid leading questions—if you are trying to get your partner to guess what's in your head, then park the idea in your notes and come back to offer it as a suggestion.
- Manage your internal voice—remember, you think faster than your partner can speak, so you might race ahead and start thinking *for* them.
- Remember that all the tips from the facilitative stance still apply here.

DIRECTIVE

A directive stance is a telling stance in which the conversation leader determines that a specific change or action is required. These conversations tend to occur when a leader is compelled to give a directive to correct a misaligned behavior or attitude, for example, in response to a breach of health and safety protocol or toxic behavior in a team. In short, there is no choice about what must change. There are also situations where a directive stance means giving direct advice. Giving advice is different from sharing, in that the leader's advice implies limited choice and advocates a specific way forward. The leader is telling their partner what they should do rather than sharing ideas for what they *could* do. Situations where direct advice may be required include times when our conversation partner is struggling to deal with a challenging situation that they have not faced before.

DIRECTIVE STANCE TIPS

- When possible, plan for the conversation and be clear about your intent.
- Get straight to the point—"I'm concerned that…" or "I need to speak to you about…"
- Refer to agreed-on expectations or processes where appropriate.
- Aim for awareness, acceptance, and action.
- Be prepared to move to a dialogical or facilitative stance when your partner accepts the need for change.
- Remain open to learning something new about the situation and be willing to adjust your position on it.
- Always agree on next steps and follow up.

The facilitative and dialogical stances consciously keep our partner in the metaphorical driver's seat. As indicated in Figure 3.2, these stances are most coach-like because they position our conversation partner as the key thinker and decision maker in the exchange. They are a genuine partner in the conversation, and we are not telling them what to do. When we move to the directive stance, on the other hand, we are telling our partner to move out of the driver's seat as we take control, at least for a while.

Above all, in this book we wish to demonstrate how leaders at all levels in a school can become better conversation leaders. When this expertise is spread across a school or system, the result is a collaborative learning culture where leaders consciously show up in more supportive ways for others. They accomplish this by studying and mastering some key communication strategies and approaches used by coaches in a range of conversational contexts—the subject matter of subsequent chapters.

PUTTING IT INTO PRACTICE

Take a moment to reflect on the questions below in relation to the concept of a continuum of conversations and the notion of stance as a conversation leader.

- When someone asks you for help or they seem to need it, how do you typically respond?
- What is driving your response?
- Considering the continuum of conversations (Figure 3.1), where do you spend most of your time in your current role?
- Thinking about the three stances, do you have a default stance?
- How might your responses change in specific conversational contexts or situations, such as more formal scheduled review and development conversations or informal, in-the-moment conversations in the hallway?
- How would you like these conversations to be positioned, and what would you expect to be noticing more of as a result?

CHAPTER 4

The Learning Conversations Map

> *"All leaders are leading language communities. Though every person, in any setting, has some opportunity to influence the nature of the existing language rules, leaders have exponentially greater access and opportunity to shape, alter or ratify."*
> **ROBERT KEGAN AND LISA LAHEY (2002)**

The previous chapter introduced a continuum of conversations (Figure 3.1) and the stances a conversation leader might adopt in service of their conversation partner's thinking and progress (Figure 3.2). As conversation leaders, the stances we adopt respond to what we perceive as our conversation partner's needs as well as our own expectations and intentions. Since learning conversations can take place in a range of settings and situations, we must also take into account the context of the conversation. The meaning of *context* as we use the term in this book encompasses the level of formality of the conversation. For example, consider the differences between a formal performance review in your office and an impromptu conversation taking place in the parking lot of your school.

In the Learning Conversations Map (Figure 4.1), the horizontal axis represents our earlier continuum of learning conversations, but now a vertical axis has been added to depict the degree of formality of the context for the conversation.

The Learning Conversations Map helps us identify and categorize the range of conversational contexts (from formal to informal) in which a leader aims to intentionally support the learning of another. A high level of formality typically means that the conversation is part of a structured process such as a one-to-one annual performance review meeting or other routine group or team meeting. These more formal conversations, which tend to fall in the upper half of the map, generally occur in a private space, often have a predetermined agenda, and are scheduled on a particular date within a particular timeframe. By contrast, conversations that fall in the bottom half of the map are more often unplanned, less formal, and relatively brief, as in the parking lot example. As we saw in the Chapter 1 vignette, these brief, less formal conversations are commonplace in the daily lives of school leaders.

FIGURE 4.1
The Learning Conversations Map:
Two Axes and Four Quadrants

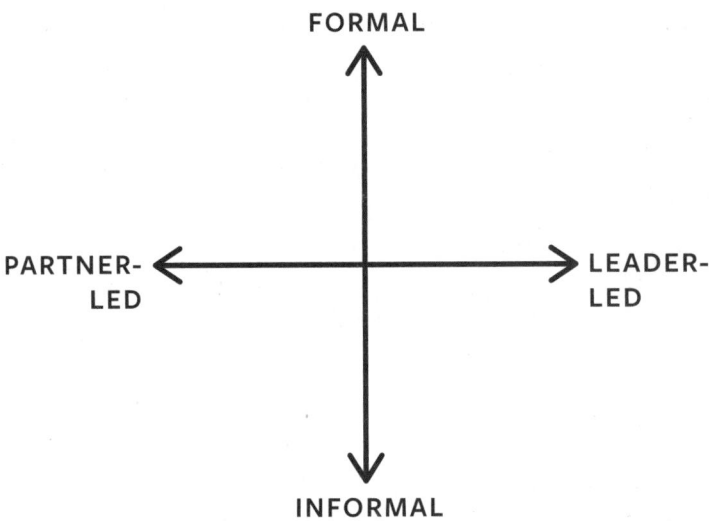

Leaders can use the map to identify opportunities to lead conversations with their colleagues that fit the context and enable effective learning to take place. For example, while formal performance review meetings serve an evaluative function, skilled conversation leaders can also frame them as opportunities for learning, growth, and progress. Figure 4.2 presents the Learning Conversations Map in more detail based on a four-quadrant matrix originally proposed by Campbell and Pascoe (2020). It highlights the relationship between the initiation and leadership of the conversation and the degree of formality of the context or process within which that conversation might be conducted.

FIGURE 4.2
The Learning Conversations Map:
Contexts of Learning Conversations

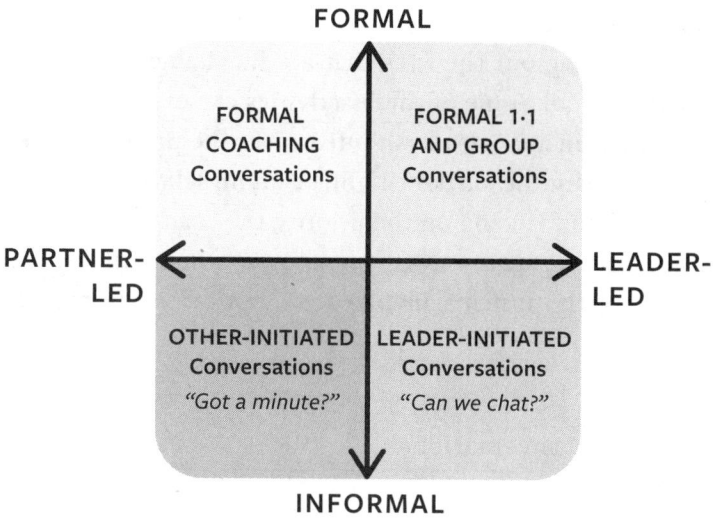

THE FOUR CONTEXTS OF LEARNING CONVERSATIONS

FORMAL COACHING CONVERSATIONS

Formal coaching conversations reside in the top-left quadrant (see Figure 4.3) because they

- Tend to be scheduled in advance;
- Are extended in time (45+ minutes per session);
- Are guided by a formal agreement that defines the boundaries of the coaching partnership;
- Are enacted over the course of multiple sessions; and
- Employ tracking systems to measure progress toward agreed-upon objectives.

Despite their "formality," most coaching conversations fall toward the partner-led end of the continuum because coachees (conversation partners) typically occupy the driver's seat; that is, they choose the focus of the coaching inquiry, set their own goals, and take steps to make progress toward meeting these goals. This is the case even when goals might be set within agreed strategic school priorities. For example, a strategic priority of an urban high school is building strong relationships with families and community. The coachee (in this case, the school principal) wants to make time to reach out to family members and community leaders and better understand their priorities but always seems to be consumed by routine activities and putting out the fires that are inevitable in the day-to-day operations of a school. Some of these activities can easily be delegated to members of the principal's leadership team, yet the principal is reluctant to delegate. ("If I want the job done right, I do it myself.") Once this is identified as a barrier to focusing on the priority, the coaching goals could be about learning to delegate in ways that empower others, utilize the skills of the team, and keep the principal involved as the priority to be progressed.

FIGURE 4.3
Formal Coaching Conversations

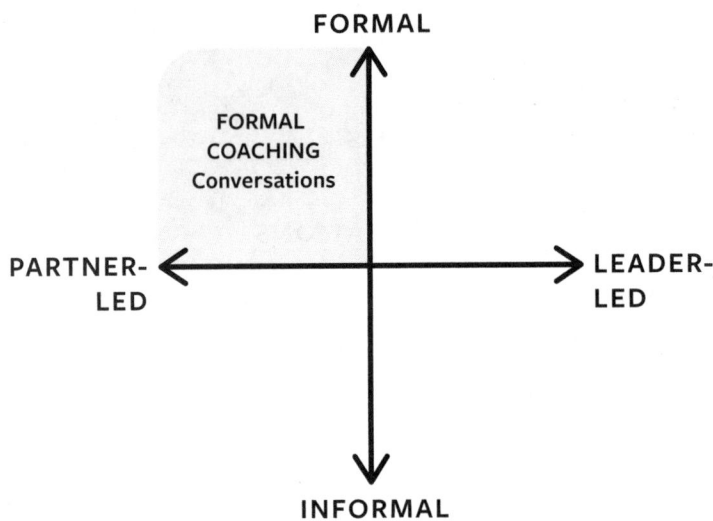

Even though the coach (conversation leader) asks questions, listens intently, shares knowledge where appropriate, and manages the conversation, the coachee is the primary decision maker and action taker. We subscribe to the following definition of coaching that occurs in this quadrant, proposed by coaching expert Christian van Nieuwerburgh (2012):

> *A one-to-one conversation that focuses on the enhancement of learning and development through increasing self-awareness and a sense of personal responsibility, where the coach facilitates the self-directed learning*

of the coachee through questioning, active listening, and appropriate challenge in a supportive and encouraging climate. (p. 17)

This definition highlights the importance of the coachee's self-direction in these kinds of conversations. It also emphasizes the role of the coach as a facilitator who applies specific skills to support the coachee's learning and progress. Importantly, van Nieuwerburgh's use of "appropriate challenge" suggests a focus on increasing the coachee's awareness of new patterns of thinking and behaving that will help them set and make progress toward goals.

FORMAL 1-1 AND GROUP CONVERSATIONS

The characteristics of conversations that sit in the top-right quadrant (see Figure 4.4) are similar to those in the top-left quadrant of the map with respect to level of formality; however, the distinction here is that conversation leaders may, initially at least, be more hands-on in terms of their leadership and management of the conversation. The similarities include the following:

- Scheduled rather than impromptu meetings.
- Level of formality (in this case, typically in the form of a predetermined agenda or process).
- A progress (or performance) monitoring component.
- Meetings that often take place in regularly scheduled intervals.

We include scheduled team meetings and working group sessions in this quadrant because they share these similarities and typically have designated leaders who lead and manage the conversations. However, we feel compelled to add an important qualifier: When we state that these contexts are more leader-led, we don't mean to imply that the leader is always the one dictating the direction and outcomes of the conversation. In fact, the leader's initial approach is likely to involve directing proceedings and keeping the agenda moving, but their stance may switch back and forth between facilitative and dialogical throughout the meeting. Further, when a meeting requires the leader to give performance feedback to the conversation partner, they may start with a directive stance but, as the conversation progresses, their stance can shift to dialogical and even facilitative. For example, in the case of a formal 1-1 annual performance review, leaders initiate, schedule, and plan the conversation with a very clear purpose and structured agenda. However, in such conversations, the lines between coaching and management can blur, since both the conversation leader and the partner stand to benefit when the leader applies the skills of active listening and powerful questioning while, at the same time, being clear about desired outcomes and next steps. This is a balancing act; however, leaders who become adept at adjusting their levels of management and contribution as well as changing stance to meet the shifting needs of the conversation can better navigate contentious conversations.

FIGURE 4.4
Formal 1-1 and Group Conversations

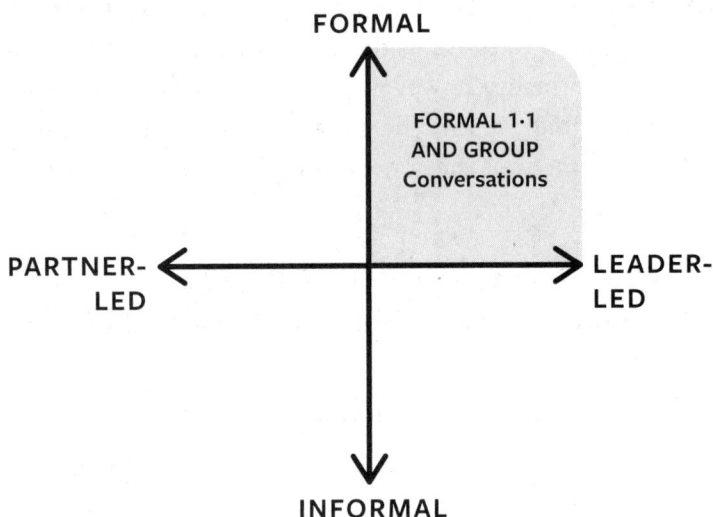

LEADER-INITIATED CONVERSATIONS

In leader-initiated conversations, positioned in the bottom-right quadrant (see Figure 4.5), the topic or agenda and timing of the conversation are proposed by the leader. Such conversations may be planned or more spontaneous in response to an emerging issue or opportunity that the leader sees. They are typically less formal, briefer, and have a clear purpose. The purpose of the conversation could be to stimulate dialogue on a particular topic or issue or simply to check in on progress with agreed tasks and outcomes. For example, leaders may wish to raise awareness and/or generate new insights for their conversation partners. In such cases, they may open the conversation by sharing information or offering a perspective on something they have noticed or would like to explore or advance. Leaders can initiate such conversations with individuals, teams, or groups. We categorize these conversations as leader-led in that they are leader-initiated and begin with the leader's agenda. However, they can still be partnering conversations, as leaders and their colleagues generate and share input as well as determine specific outcomes and come to agreement on next steps.

FIGURE 4.5
Leader-Initiated Conversations

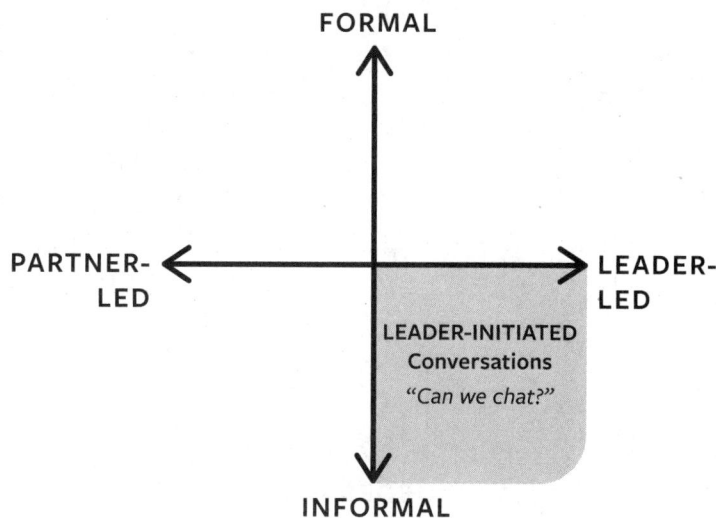

OTHER-INITIATED CONVERSATIONS

We all have experienced conversations that fall into the bottom-left quadrant in the map (see Figure 4.6). It is reserved for those unplanned, in-the-moment or "got a minute?" exchanges that we did not initiate ourselves—for example, when a colleague shares a concern or challenge and explicitly seeks your help or advice or, more subtly, starts sharing a story or experience with you without explicitly saying what they think they want or need.

These types of interactions function as learning conversations in that they offer opportunities to explore a topic, advance our partner's thinking in relation to that topic, and make progress. They are akin to what educators often call "teachable moments," and their value is maximized when leaders intentionally apply the skills and frameworks of coaching to support the thinking and progress of their conversation partner. Despite their spontaneity and brevity, even a brief conversation in a public space, such as on the sidelines of a sporting event, can present opportunities for insightful learning for both parties. The good news is that school leaders are frequently presented with such opportunities for rich and transformational learning during any given school day.

FIGURE 4.6
Other-Initiated Conversations

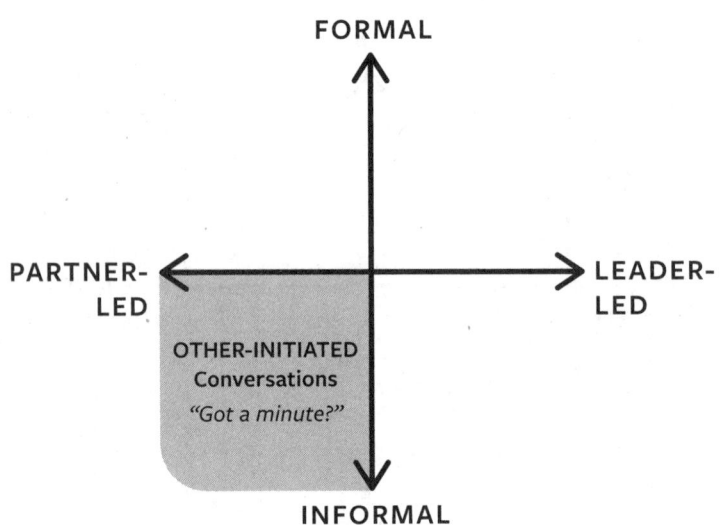

A COACHING APPROACH

Think of the Learning Conversations Map as a sensemaking tool. It will help you make sense of the myriad conversational contexts in which you engage on a day-to-day basis and identify opportunities to intentionally support the learning and progress of your conversation partners. As we have illustrated, these opportunities are not limited to the formal coaching conversations quadrant. Leaders have many more opportunities to bring a coaching approach (as opposed to being a formal coach) to their interactions in each of the other three quadrants of the map, including those that lean toward being more leader-led. We define a coaching approach as "intentionally utilizing some or all of the transferable elements of formal coaching in a range of other conversational contexts that would not typically be considered coaching interactions" (Campbell & van Nieuwerburgh, 2018, p. 18). These "transferable elements" of formal coaching include the following:

- Focusing on clarifying a desired outcome.
- Emphasizing what's wanted rather than what's not.
- Identifying resources that can assist in progressing toward and achieving the desired outcome.
- Listening and responding in ways that further our understanding and advance our conversation partner's thinking.
- Provoking insight through powerful questioning.
- Exploring options to move toward what's wanted.
- Committing to small-step actions and follow-up.
- Providing support and challenge to encourage movement and progress.
- Taking a nonevaluative stance and creating an encouraging climate.

PERSPECTIVES ON THE LEARNING CONVERSATIONS MAP: WHAT DOES IT LOOK LIKE IN YOUR ROLE?

By now, it should be clear that there are no hard boundaries around each of the quadrants of the Learning Conversations Map and that it is possible for the level of leadership and management of conversations to shift and cross from one quadrant to another, depending on how the conversations evolve. With this in mind, it can be helpful to consider the map from the perspective of different roles within an organization.

PRINCIPALS AND DISTRICT/OTHER SENIOR LEADERS

Principals and other senior leaders can engage in conversations across the whole map but will likely spend less time in the formal coaching conversations quadrant. This is in part because of the time commitment required for this kind of regular scheduled engagement but more significantly because of challenges presented by the inherent status difference if principals and other senior leaders were to formally coach those who also report to them. We previously mentioned how the lines between formal management and coaching can blur. Here we argue that, in some cases, even senior leaders can successfully undertake formal coaching cycles with their direct reports. In such situations, particular attention needs to be paid to "contracting"—cocreating an explicit agreement between the "coach" (in this case, the leader) and the "coachee" (the direct report). During this process, both parties discuss, clarify, and establish the expectations and boundaries of the coaching relationship. Moreover, leaders must learn to temper their "leader voice" and maintain psychological safety for the direct reports who have entered into coaching agreements with them. Ultimately, however, in most cases, the learning conversations of principals and senior leaders will sit predominantly in the other three quadrants.

Principals and district-level leaders are responsible for leading numerous formal conversations (top-right quadrant) with individuals and groups. They can enact these conversations in various contexts, including formal performance appraisal meetings, annual review and goal-setting processes, team meetings, working groups, and other formal meetings with members of the school community. They also engage in leader-initiated conversations (bottom-right quadrant) such as brief check-in conversations with team members, lead planning meetings with individuals or groups, and offer timely feedback on something they have become aware of. These "Can we chat?" conversations are intended to build awareness and provide opportunities to draw attention to both strengths and areas for development. Leaders use these opportunities to build and maintain momentum, keep the focus on collective goals and projects, and otherwise keep the organization moving in a positive direction.

As we saw in the vignette at the start of Chapter 1, leaders also engage in other-initiated or "got a minute?" conversations. These conversations, while unpredictable, can occur with some frequency in a variety of settings and can be initiated by many different stakeholders, for example, a parent at the school gate, a colleague on yard duty, a member of the leadership team in the hallway, or a teacher paying an impromptu visit to their principal's office. The topic of these conversations could be any aspect of school life!

MIDDLE LEADERS

Middle leaders is a broad term covering heads of departments or faculty, special education or multilingual learner coordinators, lead teachers, and similar positions of responsibility. In many ways, people in these roles are closer to the action and can be more readily accessible than senior leaders. As such, they might engage in every quadrant of the map. For example, if they have undertaken formal coaching training, they may engage in formal coaching conversations with team members or others. Middle leaders also lead in their area of responsibility through 1-1 and group conversations with direct reports and other middle leaders. They are more likely to hold annual review and goal-setting meetings as line managers of team members but less likely to be involved in formal appraisal processes or highly directive performance management conversations. Many of the learning conversations led by middle leaders are likely to fall in the bottom two quadrants of the map. They frequently interact with team members, peers, and senior leaders as well as students and parents. Any of these interactions can become a learning conversation and, like the conversations enacted by principals and other senior leaders, they can take place in a variety of settings, including during nonteaching activities. For example, a colleague may share a story of a lesson or seek advice on how to manage a challenging situation. In the leader-initiated conversations quadrant, a department head might invite dialogue with a member of their professional learning community (PLC) regarding progress toward a particular team objective. Similarly, middle leaders may seize these opportunities to raise colleagues' awareness by sharing a new development or insight.

INSTRUCTIONAL COACHES

Some may think of dedicated instructional coaches as middle leaders, but the specific nature of their role means that they spend the bulk of their time in the top-left quadrant of the map. International expert and originator of the term Jim Knight succinctly defines "instructional coaching" as partnering with teachers to help them improve teaching and learning so students become more successful (Knight, 2016, p. 2). Ideally, instructional coaches have been trained to engage in formal coaching cycles and are positioned as partners for teachers. Their purpose is to provide support, and the professional learning they provide is separate from any formal evaluative or performance appraisal process. For this reason, instructional coaches would not normally be involved in conversations that sit in the top-right quadrant of the map (i.e., formal review and development conversations) although they may lead teams such as PLCs. An instructional coach who has established credibility and trust with teachers might expect to encounter many impromptu "got a minute?" opportunities. Similarly, a coach may initiate a conversation (bottom-right quadrant) in response to an identified need that falls outside of their formal coaching function. For example, the coach might invite a teacher or team of teachers to a co-planning session with a view to improving the process of collaborative lesson planning. During this coach-initiated session, the coach may observe and offer insights on the planning process and adopt a dialogical stance to support the team toward greater clarity and alignment in their approach. These leader-initiated conversations can arise out of the broad view of practice afforded to an instructional coach in their work with numerous teachers and teams.

TEACHERS AS CONVERSATION LEADERS

In Chapter 2, we emphasized that bringing a coaching approach to conversations need not be limited to those in formal leadership positions. In the final chapter of the book, we elaborate on this point in response to a provocative and important question: What if our schools and districts were grounded in a culture of coaching in which *everyone* is a better conversation leader?

With this greater goal in mind, teachers can play an important role in normalizing learning conversations in their classrooms and schools; after all, teachers are the resident learning experts in a school. They are in a prime position to lead or participate in learning conversations in all four quadrants of our map with a broad array of conversation partners. These conversations can be teacher-to-teacher, between teacher and other professional colleagues (e.g., administrators, paraprofessionals or mental health specialists), teacher-to-parent and, perhaps most significantly, with one or more students. Just as with those in designated positions of leadership, these conversations occur in a broad range of contexts.

In the formal coaching conversations quadrant, teachers can apply coaching skills in conversations with students aimed at goal setting and monitoring students' progress. Not only do such conversations support student achievement but, when well executed, they can also enhance student agency. Also, two teachers with coaching expertise might engage in peer-to-peer coaching cycles to set and make progress toward instructional objectives. This application of coaching skills can enhance and elevate the rigor of routine peer observation and collaborative processes that already exist in many schools.

In the top-right quadrant (formal 1-1 and group conversations), individual teachers typically don't initiate or lead performance conversations with their peers, but they may lead such conversations with students and parents or caregivers. In the case of students, teachers can apply their coaching skills to conversations focused on setting academic or social-emotional goals as well as tracking progress toward these outcomes. Teachers can also bring these skills to formal parent-teacher conferences, which provide opportunities for a parent/caregiver to learn about their child's goals and how to support their child's progress toward meeting them. Conversely, teachers can learn a great deal about their students' strengths and areas of need through the use of powerful questions.

In the bottom-right quadrant, teachers may initiate conversations with students, parents, or other colleagues in less formal contexts to maintain progress on shared goals or to provide a perspective or helpful information in the moment. We regularly see evidence of a ripple effect where teachers learn about formal coaching and begin to apply their learning in more general interactions with students, colleagues, and community members in and out of classroom contexts.

Finally, in the bottom-left quadrant, learning conversations can arise in a wide range of situations. For example, teachers can be an enormous source of support to their peers simply by providing an empathetic ear. Along these lines, a teacher might seek impromptu advice from a more experienced peer in the staff room after a lesson "goes terribly wrong" or after an "uncomfortable" exchange with a parent. The contexts for these conversations may be less formal, but that doesn't make them less impactful. Similarly, in-the-moment ("got a minute?") conversations initiated by students may occur outside of the normal classroom setting—for example, at a school social event or in the schoolyard.

There are many excellent guides on how to undertake formal coaching (the top-left quadrant of the map). There are equally useful resources that cover formal performance reviews and developmental goal setting and progress monitoring (the top-right quadrant). Our intent is not to provide a comprehensive manual on formal coaching or line-management processes but to build on the knowledge base for the skills, techniques, and attributes of effective coaches and apply those to less formal conversational contexts. If we accept the premise of coaching as a way of leading, we appreciate the value of acquiring the coaching skills that make us more effective conversation leaders in these contexts—the subject matter of the following chapters.

PUTTING IT INTO PRACTICE

In Chapter 1, we invited you to go back to your diary or calendar for the past month or term and reflect on all the conversations that you had. Who were your conversation partners (e.g., parents, peers, direct reports, team members)? What was the purpose of the conversation? What was the context or setting of the conversation (i.e., was it more formal or less formal)?

Now, after being introduced to the Learning Conversations Map, where would you place each of these conversations with respect to your level of management of the conversation and the level of formality?

As you place the conversations on the map, consider any movement or positioning toward one end or another on the axes. You may find that you want to position some conversations in different or multiple quadrants depending on specific factors.

Now that you have mapped these conversations, think about what you might have done differently with respect to stance and context. For example, there may be tensions between how you would have liked the conversations to be and how they were.

What new conversations and contexts come to mind?

02
The Tools and Techniques of Coaching

Chapter 5. Bringing Shape to Conversations:
   The GROWTH Framework

Chapter 6. Fueling Conversations: Key Skills

Chapter 7. Showing Up in Conversations:
   A Coaching Way of Being

CHAPTER 5

Bringing Shape to Conversations: The GROWTH Framework

> *"All coaching conversations are either explicitly or implicitly goal focused."*
> ANTHONY GRANT (2012)

In Part 1, we made the case for coaching as a way of leading and explored some key frameworks and their related concepts:

- A continuum of conversations (partner-led to leader-led) and three stances adopted by effective conversation leaders.
- The Learning Conversations Map, which elaborates on the continuum by identifying and organizing the range of conversational contexts—informal to formal—in which we can apply a coaching approach.

Now, in Part 2, we will consider some of the specific skills and techniques used to manage formal coaching conversations that can also be utilized in less formal conversational contexts.

As an educator, you are most likely already a highly competent communicator. Think about it: Most of our vital work depends upon good communication, most often in the form of conversations with a diverse range of people in a wide range of contexts. The next few chapters are intended to help increase your self-awareness and expand your repertoire of communication skills in ways that help you to be a more effective conversation leader.

THE GROWTH FRAMEWORK

The GROWTH framework (Campbell, 2016a) is a research-informed conversational framework that has been used by thousands of educators for more than two decades. It brings greater intentionality and shape to the range of conversations depicted in the Learning Conversations Map and, when well executed, gives your conversation partner a sense of forward momentum. Developed initially by Mandy O'Bree, one of the founders of GCI, the GROWTH framework (Figure 5.1) is an elaboration of the GROW model popularized by leadership development expert Sir John Whitmore and his colleagues in the 1980s and 1990s (Whitmore, 1992). GROWTH is not only an easy-to-remember acronym, but it is also easy to apply. In Whitmore's original model, the G stands for goal; R for reality; O for options; and W for will. We have elaborated on GROW with the addition of the T (tactics) and H (habits) to help ensure that conversations move beyond good intentions to actions by positioning our conversation partners for success. The GROWTH framework is a core element of GCI's approach to coach development and has served as an effective framework for educators in a wide range of formal and informal settings.

Before describing each stage of the framework, we need to offer an important disclaimer: While the framework suggests a logical, step-by-step progression, learning conversations are rarely linear. The GROWTH framework is not intended to operate as a six-question script or lockstep formula, although, in some instances, using it that way might lead to very satisfying outcomes! Instead, think of it as a gentle guide, or series of signposts, that helps the conversation leader manage the conversation more effectively, ultimately leading to more productive outcomes. We will return to this idea in the discussion of loops and cycles later in this chapter.

The framework calls upon conversation leaders to pose questions clustered around the areas signified by each letter of the GROWTH acronym. It is intended to increase your awareness of your conversation partner's thinking and, when possible, support them in arriving at their own methods and solutions to achieve the goals that they have articulated.

G IS FOR GOAL: WHAT'S WANTED?

This part of the framework is about your conversation partner's desired outcomes or their *preferred future*, a term that is used in solution-focused coaching. Solutions-focused (SF) theory (Jackson & McKergow, 2007) suggests that we can best approach problems or surmount challenges by defining—in detail—what is wanted instead. Once we have painted a clear and compelling picture of the preferred future, we can then focus on ways to move toward it.

FIGURE 5.1
The GROWTH Framework

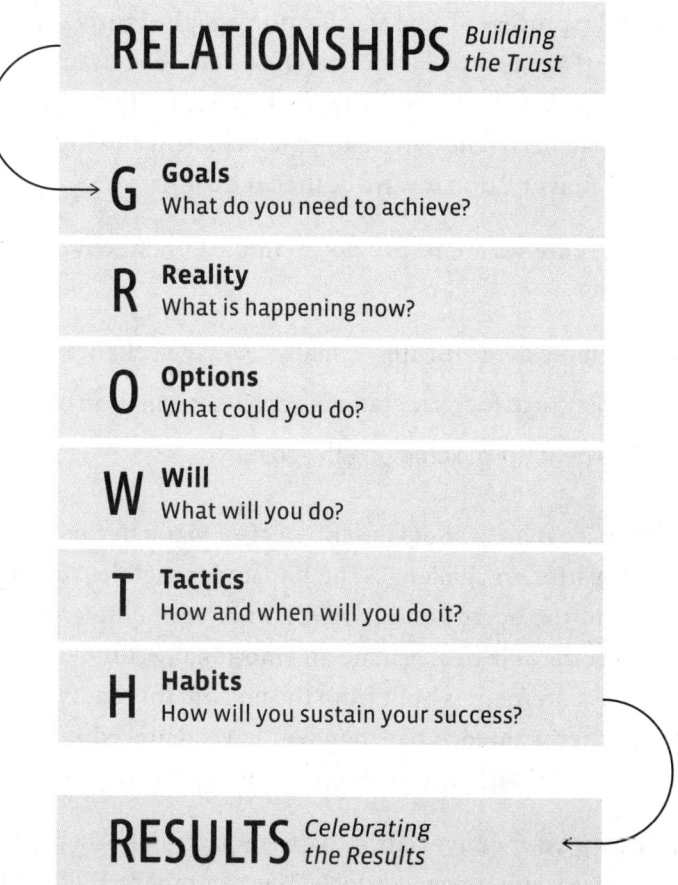

Source: From J. Campbell, 2016a. In C. van Nieuwerburgh (Ed.), *Coaching in Professional Contexts* (pp. 235–240). Used with permission.

It may seem counterintuitive, but digging around for causes and spiraling around what's *not* wanted is not necessarily helpful and often slows progress toward what *is* wanted. Think about your own responses to challenging situations and circumstances. Have you ever found yourself so preoccupied with what you don't want that you never actually thought about what it is you do want? While this is a common phenomenon, a good conversation leader can frame the conversation in a manner that brings attention to what *is* wanted instead.

Reframing can be a powerful catalyst for progress. In *The Art of Framing: Managing the Language of Leadership* (1996), Fairhurst and Sarr propose that conversation leaders can be helpful framers or, more often perhaps, reframers. We can help shift our conversation partner from feeling stuck in the present by reorienting the conversation to the future. This shift in perception also furthers the process of goal clarification and the motivation to change the status quo (Fairhurst & Sarr, 1996). Of course, the reframing should be undertaken respectfully, meaning that we listen to and empathize with our conversation partner as they articulate their challenge before we rush into reframing the conversation toward desired outcomes.

The following sentence stems provide a simple but effective way to define and clarify goals:

- *By…* [a timeframe in the future—usually several weeks or months].
- *I am/have…* [a future-focused statement of what will be in place].
- *So that…* [the benefits of achieving the goal].

The last stem ("so that") should describe a clear, attractive endpoint in relation to the situation or challenge. The impact is tangible! You are likely to witness a lift in the energy and motivation of your conversation partner when they become able to articulate an emotionally compelling goal. Preferably, the goal statement is built from the bottom up, that is, what the conversation partner wanted, what they will have achieved in getting those things, and when they hope to get there.

When you help your conversation partners articulate their goals in this way, they begin to define *approach* goals (the attainment of what they want) rather than *avoidance* goals (the avoidance of what they don't want). This is a welcome change, as research has shown that approach goals are positively associated with increased self-efficacy, motivation, and well-being (Braunstein & Grant, 2016).

GOING DEEPER INTO GOAL-SETTING THEORY

Professor Anthony Grant of the University of Sydney was a leading academic in the world of coaching psychology, and his influence has been far-reaching. According to Grant (2012), coaches need a deeper and more nuanced understanding of goals so that we can help our coachees formulate goals that they really strive to reach. He summarizes five broad types of goal:

Avoidance and approach: Avoidance goals are expressed as movement away from an undesirable state. Approach goals, on the other hand, are expressed as a movement toward a specific (positive) state or outcome. Approach goals help to define appropriate goal-striving behaviors and have been shown to increase performance and well-being. The opposite has been found for long-term pursuit of avoidance goals.

Performance and learning: Performance goals tend to focus on task execution and measurable performance. These can be very motivating when early success is possible. However, they can be demotivating and impede performance when the task is highly complex, the stakes are high, or the necessary skills, resources, or self-efficacy are limited.

Learning (mastery): These goals focus on the learning associated with a task rather than the performance of the task itself. They are associated with more positive cognitive and emotional processes, enhanced memory and well-being, and enhanced individual performance in complex or challenging situations.

Proximal and distal: These terms refer to the time-framing of goals and perceptions of attainability. *Proximal* goals are shorter term and tend to stimulate more detailed action planning. *Distal* goals are longer-term—"a broad fuzzy vision." Combination is the key.

Self-concordant: This refers to the degree to which a goal is aligned with an individual's intrinsic interests, motivations, and values. This aspect presents a tension stemming from the coachee's perception of the degree to which their goals are self- or externally directed, which, in turn, has a bearing on levels of motivation, engagement, and satisfaction.

R IS FOR REALITY AND RESOURCES: WHAT'S HAPPENING NOW AND WHAT'S HELPING?

We first need to understand our conversation partner's current situation (the "reality") before we can begin to support their progress toward their desired outcome. They may already have access to resources that will help them narrow the gap between their present reality and desired state.

Therefore, the R in the GROWTH framework reminds us to search for strengths that can support goal attainment. At times, these strengths are not obvious to our conversation partner, so we need to deliberately probe for them. When conversation leaders help their partners uncover and be mindful of such resources, they further the partner's *agency thinking*, that is, the belief that goal attainment is within their reach as well as the motivation to take action. Shane Lopez, a psychologist and expert on hope, affirmed that agency thinking can enhance levels of hope in a powerful way (Lopez, 2013). Lopez further defined agency as "our perceived ability to shape our lives day by day" (p. 25).

When we struggle to overcome vexing challenges, we can get mired in the negative dimensions of our current reality to the point that we are no longer able to envision the possibility of a better future. But when conversation leaders gently challenge their partners' depiction of the current reality, they can help them move beyond narratives of helplessness and hopelessness. Skilled conversation leaders can help sharpen their partner's understanding of the current reality by asking focused questions such as:

- "What successes have you had thus far?"
- "What personal or professional strengths can you draw from to meet the challenge?"
- "Who else on your team can support you in your efforts?"

We use these types of questions to direct attention to any evidence of progress (no matter how small) and to help our conversation partner clarify what is already working. In doing so, we help them restore a sense of resourcefulness and possibility that can lead them to articulate their preferred future. When they are able to clearly articulate both their current reality and their better future, our conversation partner is ready to consider possible courses of action, or options.

O IS FOR OPTIONS: EXPLORING POSSIBILITIES: WHAT COULD YOU DO?

So, we now have a compelling goal expressed as a "preferred future" along with a clearer picture of the current reality, including what has already been accomplished and is already in place. A logical next question is "How will we get there?" The Options phase of the framework gives specific attention to generating new ways to bring our conversation partner closer to achieving the goal. More specifically, we work to move our conversation partner beyond being stuck by helping them identify options within their sphere of influence that will help them achieve their desired outcomes. We accomplish this through the use of intentional questions that invite consideration of a range of possible ways forward.

When exploring possibilities, conversation leaders will have to determine the most appropriate stance based on their conversation partner's needs and the context of the conversation. In other words, you will either refrain from offering suggestions or offer them provisionally. Since agency thinking enhances hope and motivation, when possible, make space for your conversation partner to formulate their own options (sticking with a facilitative stance). Although it can be tempting to jump to a dialogical stance and unleash some of your know-how, this isn't necessarily the best way to motivate your partner to take action. However, there are times when it may be more expedient or helpful to share some options, particularly if your partner knows you have knowledge related to their topic and asks you to do share. You should always seek their permission before offering any suggestions (e.g., "Would you like me to share some options that I've seen work in the past?"). (We will look closely at the skill of sharing knowledge and perspective in Chapter 6.) If the conversation partner agrees, be sure to invite them to apply any suggestions you make to their own context and adapt them as needed. Remember, a dialogical stance is not about telling our partner what to do; it is about sharing in ways that enable choice. This also reinforces their sense of ownership and, with this, their responsibility to take action. Whitmore (2009) sums this up well: "If I give you advice and it fails, you will blame me. I have traded my advice for your responsibility, and that is seldom a good deal" (p. 37).

Just as agency thinking contributes to our partner's hopefulness, so does *pathways thinking*, defined by Lopez (2013) as the ability to find "routes around obstacles that stand in our way" (p. 19). Indeed, there seems to be a cyclical relationship between agency thinking and pathways thinking—one feeds upon the other (Figure 5.2).

As our conversation partner conceives of alternate pathways, they are closer to making positive decisions about what to do in their context—the next phase of our framework.

W IS FOR WILL: DECISION TIME! WHAT WILL YOU DO?

Great ideas won't get you very far unless you act on them! After we move out of the exploratory thinking of the Options phase, the conversation pivots toward action. It is decision time, and our overarching question is "What will you do?" There are different ways to frame this question, some of which help to gauge engagement; for example, "Which of these ideas excite or energize you the most?" Here, the shape of the conversation shifts from being divergent (idea generation) to being more convergent (working through the ideas toward the best way forward).

FIGURE 5.2
Agency Thinking, Pathways Thinking, and Hope

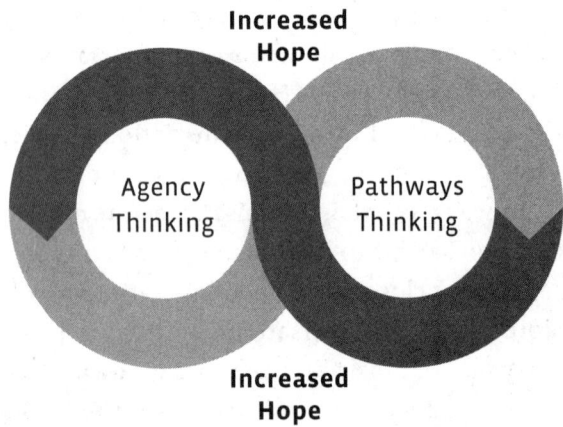

Source: Adapted from J. Campbell and C. van Nieuwerburgh, *The Leader's Guide to Coaching in Schools: Creating Conditions for Effective Learning*, p. 55, 2018. Used with permission.

Too many leadership conversations stop here, when the leader feels that they moved their conversation partner to committing to action. However, when the conversation concludes without a sufficient level of clarity and precision about what the person will do next, the W could stand for wishful thinking! For this reason, we added the Tactics (T) and Habits (H) phases to dramatically increase the likelihood of transforming good intentions into great results!

T IS FOR TACTICS: LET'S GET SPECIFIC!

As we established in the prior section, good intentions are no guarantee of forward momentum or success. Assuming that your conversation partner has expressed the will to commit to action, how will you ensure that they will follow through? The Tactics phase is about articulating the precise details of what our conversation partner will do, including when, where, how, and with whom. Both parties may find this phase challenging or even slightly uncomfortable (think back to the times you've been asked questions like "When do you think you'll finish this report?"). However, if we have already built a positive and supportive relationship with our partner, they will be better prepared (and more likely) to commit to their plan if they have clarified its specific details. At this point, gaining commitment to small-step actions is helpful and vital. In fact, it is often beneficial for the conversation partner to record their small-step actions, thereby further increasing responsibility and supportive accountability.

H IS FOR HABITS: FOLLOWING THROUGH AND SUSTAINING SUCCESS

Your conversation partner has now committed to some short-term actions toward achieving their goal. So, how can you help them ensure sustainability? Think about your New Year's resolutions: On January 1, you resolved to stay healthy with a daily exercise routine and adhered to it strictly for the first month. By February, you succumbed to the inevitable invitations to join your colleagues for happy hour drinks and nibbles after work. By March, you have abandoned the program entirely. Does this sound familiar?

In retrospect, what would have helped you stick to the program? Perhaps, if you had had the foresight (and money) to hire a personal trainer, your routine would have become habitual. In a similar way, you can help your conversation partner progress toward meeting long-term goals by prompting them to consider the resources and supports that will sustain their momentum and make their early successes habitual. You don't need to belabor this process, but if your conversation partner thinks ahead to the resources, attitudes, and supports that will help them stay the course (both in the short and longer term), they are more likely to attain success. Sometimes, all it takes is asking a single, simple question like "How can we build in support for your ongoing progress toward your goal?"

HOLDING THE FRAMEWORK LIGHTLY: LOOPS, CYCLES, AND FLEXIBILITY

Think back to our previous qualifier: *Learning conversations are rarely linear.* The visual presentation of the GROWTH framework (Figure 5.1) may suggest a structure that is rigidly sequenced. And while there is some rationale for following the process closely during a formal coaching conversation,

conversation leaders often use the framework flexibly and with a light touch. In other words, our conversation partner will not necessarily follow the signposts in a linear order. That said, the signposts can be used to manage the direction of the conversation—they can help you gauge where your conversation partner is in their thinking and how ready they are to make progress. A conversation might commence with your conversation partner expressing dissatisfaction with their current reality, for example, a principal who tells you "I'm overwhelmed by all these Central Office initiatives that keep hitting me while I'm trying to run a school." In response, you might offer prompts that redirect the conversation in a manner that helps your long-suffering principal formulate a motivating and actionable goal about them regaining more control (feeling less overwhelmed). Another example might be a teacher who chose a course of action ("I started the lesson by trying to engage students in inquiry and asking a lot of questions") that didn't pan out ("No response at all. I lost them in the first five minutes"). In this instance, the appropriate action could be to tactfully loop back to O (Options) to focus the conversation on alternative courses of action. ("I understand how this could be frustrating. Even the most experienced teachers have lessons that fall flat. When we spoke earlier you mentioned that there are some instances in which direct instruction might be a better course of action. Could this have been one of those cases?") It could also be useful to revisit the goal to check that it is still relevant and compelling for the teacher and aligns with the strategy that they attempted to implement.

Typical learning conversations tend to include several loops, and our partner may progress across several stages of the framework as their thinking develops. Typically, however, much more time is spent cycling around G-R-O than on the more convergent phases of W-T-H. Options can pop up at any stage in the conversation, and a skilled conversation leader will hold the framework (albeit lightly) in a manner that best supports their partner's thinking and progress.

A CONVERSATION BUILT ON TRUST

As we have seen, the use of a snappy acronym does not automatically result in an effective coaching conversation. In the case of the GROWTH framework, think of it as a helpful set of signposts that bring shape and direction to conversations. It could be said that the use of a conversational framework such as GROWTH helps to maintain the structural integrity of the conversation as it builds with increasing clarity and momentum toward change. Taking this analogy one step further, the foundation on which this framework stands (or wobbles!) is a relationship based on mutual trust. Without trust, rooted in authentic engagement and investment in our conversation partner, the conversation runs the risk of becoming more transactional than transformational.

SIMPLE BUT NOT SIMPLISTIC

While the GROWTH framework can appear deceptively simple, as you begin to apply it to your own conversations, you will soon discover that the shift from transactional to transformational conversations often requires a high level of skill. Similar to what has been written about the skills that coaches use, conversation skills aren't something we are born with; they must be learned and practiced:

> *In defining coaching as a form of 'conversation' it can be easy to trivialise and underplay the critical importance of effective coaching skill development training. Coaching is a specific kind of conversation, full of intention; subtle and not so subtle shifts in perspective; carefully nuanced language; and acutely refined listening among other things. (Campbell, 2016b, p. 140)*

Chapter 6 is devoted to key skills that support learning conversations. And, while such "technical" skills are valuable, the manner in which you show up in conversations is equally important. For example, if you find it difficult to empathize with your conversation partner, even the most skillfully executed prompts or moves won't get you far. For this reason, we have devoted a full chapter (Chapter 7) to showing up.

In conclusion, GROWTH is not a type of coaching. The GROWTH framework is one of three core elements of effective coaching conversations that are fueled by key skills and underpinned by our way of being, or how we show up. Learning to apply these elements to your daily conversations takes practice, perseverance, and faith in both the process and our conversation partners. We encourage you to give yourself some grace as learners as you master a coaching approach to leadership. Getting to a 6 out of 10 in competence using the framework is fairly easy and is likely to make a noticeable positive difference to your conversations.

PUTTING IT INTO PRACTICE

Reflect on how the shape of a conversation guided by the GROWTH framework compares to your regular learning conversations with colleagues.

- What has been affirming for you as you have read the chapter?
- What has challenged or extended your thinking?
- How aware and intentional are you about how you manage the shape of conversations?
- Which stages of the framework do you feel you need to spend more or less time on in your learning conversations, and what will be the benefits of that?
- What practical strategies will help you to make use of the GROWTH signposts in upcoming learning conversations?
- What will be the small signs of success if you do this more effectively?

CHAPTER 6

Fueling Conversations: Key Skills

> *"Great conversations are generative; they allow for the creation of new images and metaphors and they change how people think."*
> JACKIE STAVROS AND CHERI TORRES (2018)

If the GROWTH framework provides a set of signposts to help us manage and bring shape to our conversations, then key skills—the subject matter of this chapter—are what fuel them. The key skills of coaching are well documented in the literature. Researchers and practitioners alike are, for the most part, in agreement on the specific skills that effective coaches apply in their coaching conversations. Our good friend and colleague Professor Christian van Nieuwerburgh is a globally recognized expert on coaching skills, and his bestselling text An Introduction to Coaching Skills: A Practical Guide (2020) is essential reading for all coaches (and mentors, for that matter).

Among many other components of effective coaching, van Nieuwerburgh proposes four key skills and explains their application in formal coaching contexts:

- Listening to encourage thinking
- Asking powerful questions
- Paraphrasing and summarizing
- Noticing

While these skills apply to both formal and informal contexts, we have learned from experience that, especially in less formal contexts, conversation leaders inevitably encounter situations that warrant sharing some of their knowledge or perspective. For this reason, we have added a fifth skill to van Nieuwerburgh's list—sharing knowledge and perspective. The skill component here is not what you bring to the conversation but how you use it. Since we spend so much time espousing the value of defaulting to a facilitative stance throughout this book, knowing when and how to share dialogically can be challenging. For this reason, we take a deep dive into this topic in the final portion of the chapter.

Finally, we want to acknowledge that most of our readers have probably drawn on many of the skills covered in this chapter because, as we've stated more than once, conversation is the lifeblood of schools and other human-intensive organizations. Given that these skills may seem like second nature, this chapter is intended to raise your level of awareness and fine-tune many of the skills that you already possess. Our aim is to help you become "consciously competent" in how you support the thinking and progress of your conversation partners.

You do not need to master all the skills at once, and you may choose to dip in and out of the chapter as you build your repertoire. We have included a checklist at the end of the chapter to assist you in reflecting on your progress.

LISTENING TO ENCOURAGE THINKING

Let's be honest: How often in our day-to-day interactions do we really listen with our full attention? In normal everyday social circumstances, we rarely interact as consciously as we do in coaching conversations. In social contexts, most of us listen at a surface level, perhaps to get some specific information, catch up on the news, or learn the background of a situation so we can comment confidently. Sometimes we don't really listen at all and just wait for our turn to talk. That is, in social circumstances, we often default to a form of listening for our own benefit.

In a coaching context, on the other hand, whether formal or informal, our listening is primarily in the service of our conversation partner: We listen to help our conversation partner grow their understanding of their current reality and how they might make progress. Our role as conversation leaders has a greater impact when we help our partner listen to themselves and tune into their own thinking. In that context, we strongly recommend that paraphrases and summaries offered by the conversation leader include the key words and references used by our conversation partner. This helps to limit the listener's tendency to do too much interpreting of what has been said. Most importantly, our conversation partner hears their thinking reflected back, often for the first time.

Armstrong (2012) captures this perfectly in this powerful coaching question:

> So, after hearing yourself tell me about this situation, what are you thinking now? (p. 37)

Not only is this a question that is likely to encourage further thinking, but it also emphasizes important points about the purpose and function of listening in coaching—listening (along with noticing) is the key skill that helps us determine our next conversational move. While listening is the most fundamental skill of the conversation leader, it can be challenging to master, especially in the brief, less formal interactions that often fill our days. When listening well, we give our full attention to our conversation partner. This may sound easy, but it's often at odds with many of our conversation habits. As author and leadership consultant Nancy Kline (2011) honestly and forthrightly puts it:

> We think we listen but we don't. We finish each other's sentences, we interrupt each other, we moan together, we fill in the pauses with our own stories, we look at our watches, we sigh, we frown, tap our finger, read, or walk away. We give advice, give advice, and give advice. (p. 37)

In her book *Time to Think* (2011), Kline introduces the concept of "thinking environments." These are spaces in which we can think for ourselves, free from the assumptions and judgments of others. In such environments, we can better approach our challenges and decisions with clarity and creativity. While Kline provides 10 components of thinking environments, the first and most important component is attention. In fact, Kline asserts that "the quality of your attention determines the quality of other people's thinking" (p. 36)—a powerful statement. Simply stated, attention is about listening to our conversation partners with an undivided focus and being present for them.

TUNING OUR LISTENING

We may listen intently with the best intentions, but if we don't know what we are listening for, we are likely to be of little support to our conversation partner. Similarly, certain listening qualities promote safety, trust, honesty and, ultimately, convey our support. "Tuning our listening" captures both the objects of our listening (what we listen *for*) and the manner in which we listen (what we listen *with*). As conversation leaders, it can be helpful to think of how we might tune our listening more intentionally. Figure 6.1 provides a graphic illustration of the things we might want to tune on our listening "radar."

FIGURE 6.1
Our Listening Radar

LISTENING FOR...

"Listening for" is about picking up on the things that will be most helpful to our conversation partner, often in amongst the "noise." A coachee once told one of us that her coaching conversations were like wearing noise-cancelling headphones. She was referring to the clarity of thinking she achieved during her sessions, a key factor of which was what the coach listened *for* as she talked about her professional world and its challenges.

In the following section, we provide guidance to help you zero in on what really matters.

Listening for What's Wanted. Conversation leaders must be attuned to their partner's needs and desires in order to be able to support them in formulating goals. We don't always have the luxury of an extended period of time to discern what is wanted, let alone a private space for the conversation. In less formal contexts, such as a brief hallway conversation, we want to get to the heart of the matter in that moment. Remember that many of us tend to lapse into a default of talking about what we don't want. In the prior chapter on the GROWTH framework, we touched upon the skill of reframing, which is especially helpful in shifting our partner's negative thinking to envisioning positive outcomes or a desired state. Here, we emphasize that sometimes we need to listen to what lies beneath the surface of our partner's words in an effort to discern their desired state even as they fixate on their current (undesirable) state. In doing so, we are better able to pose questions that seek more clarity on positive alternatives and progress.

Listening for Resources. Listening for resources is about tuning our listening to possible resources that will help our partner make progress toward their goal. Some of these resources may live within our partner, such as resilience, specialized knowledge, or experience. Others may be found in their environment, including teammates, sources of knowledge, or helpful data. And, as stated previously, drawing from their own past experience (e.g., what worked or what didn't work) can also serve as a valuable resource and catalyst of progress. For example, we may uncover resources in casual statements like "I used to do this well" or "I have a really capable team." Make a mental or physical note of such statements as the conversation progresses and return to them to enhance your conversation partner's sense of what is possible as well as to inform their options.

Listening for Strengths. Listening for strengths is about dialing up our "strengths radar" to full sensitivity! Just as we work to replace deficit thinking about our students with a strengths-based perspective, as conversation leaders, we help our partners become more solution-focused by surfacing their strengths. Once again, we may need to listen beneath the surface of their words, especially when they feel stuck or overwhelmed with a challenge. However, when we listen attentively, we can often discern strengths in the way our partners talk about their situations and challenges. For example, this might be in the passion with which they talk about wanting to be more inclusive in their practices or the empathic way that they talk about members of their team. Similarly, when they respond to your question about what has worked for them when they tackled similar situations in the past, strengths are likely to emerge. Noticing and naming these strengths and linking them back to our conversation partner's narrative not only generates helpful positive emotions but helps them feel more resourceful.

Listening for Emotions. When conversation leaders listen for emotions, they engage in a deeper form of listening. Here, we move beyond listening for information to tuning into the feelings behind the content. In doing so, we are "hearing" what is not being said—the emotional context of the words.

These emotions can be both positive—joyful, energetic, enthusiastic—and negative—frustrated, disappointed, angry, and so on. When we name these emotions, we demonstrate empathy (see below) for our conversation partner in the manner of an emotional paraphrase, communicating that we get what is happening for them.

LISTENING WITH...

Good listeners are not only hyper-aware of their conversation partner's words and emotions, but they are also self-aware. "Listening with" is about how we show up in our conversations, specifically how the way we listen contributes to our partner's thinking and progress. The four "listening with" qualities discussed below are separate but very much intertwined.

Listening with Empathy. When we listening with empathy, we dial down any judgment or ambivalence that we may be feeling as our conversation partner describes their situation. Since humans have a natural tendency to be influenced by their own biases and experiences, as listeners, we must learn to notice and manage our own internal narrative. For example, if your conversation partner describes a challenge that is reminiscent of one that you have experienced yourself, you may be tempted interrupt them with an account of how you handled it. However, in doing so, you are likely to shut down your partner and may miss an opportunity to better understand and/ or probe their reality. We can only be fully present for our partner when we are fully attuned to ourselves, including our judgments, preconceptions, and emotions. When we do this well, we come closer to truly understanding what the person is experiencing and feeling at that point in time and can respond appropriately.

Listening with Curiosity. Curiosity is a natural (and wonderful) human trait. Those who listen with curiosity are genuinely interested and open to different scenarios and possibilities. When we stay curious, we ask more thought-provoking questions and avoid the temptation to ask leading questions. Like empathy, our curiosity helps us to manage our tendency to race ahead of our conversation partner and mentally construct our own solutions to their challenge. Also, like many of our students, our conversation partners may need sufficient time to construct their thoughts and put them into words. We often don't realize that we think faster than our partners can put their thinking into words. Consequently, it is important to apply sufficient wait time and refrain from interrupting both their thinking and their articulation of their thoughts.

Listening with Respect. We may have expertise in leading learning conversations, but an important component of our expertise is recognizing that our partner is the expert in their world. When you practice this form of respectful listening, you communicate to your partner that you value their words, perspective, and capacity for thinking. Respect also means refraining from imposing your own priorities, directives, or agenda, and giving your partner the grace to think for themselves. Listening with respect liberates them to formulate their own meaningful goals, experience a greater sense of ownership, and make progress toward achieving their desired outcomes.

Listening with Humility. When we listen with humility, we put aside our expertise and position ourselves as learners. Humble listeners strive to reduce any perception of status difference between themselves and their partner. When we dial down our voice, we amplify theirs. Above all, we can signal our humility by managing our tendency to share our own stories and give advice too readily. In other words, rather than providing answers, we ask powerful questions—a skill that we address in the following section.

ASKING POWERFUL QUESTIONS

While listening is a critically important coaching skill, the art of asking questions that elicit thinking and generate insight and clarity is what distinguishes transactional conversations from those that are potentially transformative. However, as with listening, the kinds of questions we default to are not always the most helpful to our conversation partners. In the coaching literature, questions or prompts are often categorized by the intent or function of the questions, such as probing, provocative, evocative, motivational, and challenging. Significantly, each of these adjectives used to describe a type of question is associated with a verb form; for example, a probing question is intended to probe (thinking, beliefs, etc.), whereas a provocative question may provoke the listener to think about a problem in a different way.

But while these categories can be helpful, they also have their limitations, in that a well-formulated question can serve multiple purposes and lead to more than one outcome. Above all, our questions should be drivers of the thinking and progress of our conversation partner. The "power" in powerful questioning is a product of multiple components.

- **Responsive:** Powerful questions are the right question at the right time—not necessarily the next question in the script.
- **Intentional:** Powerful questions are fueled by our intentions, meaning that we ask them to achieve deliberate outcomes. At times, our intention is to encourage divergent and expansive thinking, often early in the conversation. At other stages, more convergent or precise thinking is required, for example, when our conversation partner commits to next steps.
- **Thought-provoking:** Powerful questions help generate new insights or perspectives. The purpose is to prompt our conversation partner to consider the situation from a new or novel perspective. A sign that we've asked a thought-provoking question might be the response "Hmmm, that's a good question…," followed by a "thinking silence."
- **Promoting action and accountability:** Powerful questions provide a motivating call to action for our conversation partner. We use these questions to prompt our partner to articulate their intentions in concrete detail, an action that typically stimulates a greater sense of responsibility. We often witness a lift in energy in our conversation partner as a result.
- **Real:** Powerful questions are ones that we don't know the answer to. They are not leading questions or suggestions dressed up or veiled as questions.
- **Succinct:** Powerful questions are unambiguous and get straight to the point and are allowed to land with our conversation partner without conjoined supplementary questions or rephrasing.
- **Solution-focused:** Powerful questions are solution-focused, meaning that they elicit more clarity about what is wanted, draw attention to strengths and resources, and generate a sense of possibility in our conversation partner. (More on this later.)
- **Building trust:** Powerful questions strengthen our partner's sense of safety and trust. When we ask questions that fit all the criteria above, we show that we are present, attentive, and have positive intention, all of which encourage our partner to offer more candid responses.

MOVING FROM PROBLEM-FOCUSED TO SOLUTION-FOCUSED QUESTIONS AND CONVERSATIONS

The previous chapter introduced the concept of reframing—a skill that shifts the discourse from what is *not* working to what *is* wanted.

Solution-focused questions are a powerful tool for enacting such shifts. More specifically, solution-focused inquiry helps your partner to reframe problems in ways that create movement toward their resolution. As we stated previously, we don't mean to suggest that you should minimize or ignore your partner's problem—actions that most certainly will erode their trust in you. And the last thing we want to do is silence them when they discuss their problem. Instead, we intentionally use solution-focused questions to flip our partner's thinking toward positive alternatives and possibilities and avoid using problem-focused questions that delay or prevent them from formulating solutions. Consider the problem-focused questions and their solution-focused alternatives below.

TYPICAL PROBLEM-FOCUSED QUESTIONS

Why is this such a problem? You may believe that if you and your conversation partners find the root cause of the problem, you will be more able to solve it. While this seems intuitive, as we've emphasized, this line of questioning serves only to offer more clarity on what's not wanted rather than help shift your partner's narrative to one about a more desirable future. Our all-too-human tendency to spiral on the negative not only dims our sense of hope but can also lead to blaming others and, subconsciously, abdicating our own responsibility for our undesirable status quo.

How are you feeling about this? Again, we may ask this question in the spirit of empathy, but the negative response that it invariably elicits from our partner only compounds their unhappiness. In fact, they may tell you how they are feeling without having to be prompted!

What are the difficulties you face? Again, conventional problem-solving logic might suggest that we need to know about all the difficulties and barriers (see next question) to be able to resolve the situation. Solution-focused thinking proposes that we don't need to rehash every perceived difficulty in order to make progress.

What are the barriers to overcome in relation to this? Similarly, probing barriers too early in the process can (paradoxically) create more sizeable barriers between your partner and their desired future.

Finally, problem-focused questions rarely promote deep thinking and usually just confirm (or even exaggerate) what our partner already knows.

Here are some solution-focused alternatives:

- What would you like to *achieve* in relation to this?
- If we could make *some* progress on this, how would *that* make you feel?
- If this *was working well*, what would be happening?
- When *has* there been a time, in the past, when you handled this challenge, or something similar, successfully?
- What would others notice if you were managing this challenge *well*?
- If you *could* take just one single action to move this forward, what would it be?

Some additional solution-focused questions in response to problem-talk appear in Figure 6.2.

PARAPHRASING AND SUMMARIZING

Sometimes, when learning to coach or be more coach-like as a leader, people presume that listening and questioning are the two most important skills. Early in the learning process, we may think that coaches and conversation leaders engage in a process of questioning and listening that consists of nodding one's head, acknowledging the coachee or partner's responses to questions, and perhaps taking a few notes. This description seems more like an interview than a coaching conversation in that it is missing an important function—that of clarifying. Clarifying most commonly takes the form of paraphrasing and summarizing for various purposes such as listing, organizing, and prioritizing. These skills can be every bit as powerful as a well-chosen question.

Paraphrasing and summarizing can be used to help our conversation partner clarify their thinking as well as confirm that we heard and understood them. Like listening and questioning, we use paraphrasing and summarizing to stimulate our conversation partner's thinking rather than our own.

PARAPHRASING

When we paraphrase, we present our partner's words and thoughts back to them. In this way, we afford them the opportunity to hear their thinking played back. You don't need to play back every word that your partner spoke. Instead, you can provide a paraphrase that captures their key points. To better understand the power of paraphrasing, reflect on a job interview for what seemed like a dream job. The interviewer poses a question ("What do think are your greatest strengths?"). You answer as best you can, but in a lingering moment of self-doubt (and we all have those), you want to be absolutely certain that they heard and fully understood your response and punctuate your response with words like "Does that make sense?" The interviewer could conceivably respond with a simple yes, and while that would offer you some reassurance, wouldn't it be more satisfying (and helpful) if they, instead, offered you a paraphrase that effectively captured the gist of your response?

FIGURE 6.2
Getting Unstuck with Solution-Focused Reframing Questions

Problem Talk	Solution-Focused Response
There's so much to do, I don't know where to start.	When you've been in this situation before, what helped you get back in control?
Nothing is working! Everything is going wrong.	Nothing at all is working? Tell me just one thing that is going right.
I can't think of a way to solve this.	Tell me about a time in the past when you tackled a similar challenge successfully.
I've never had this challenge before.	Who else do you know who does this well?
I've tried lots of different strategies, and it's still the same issue.	Tell me about any aspect of the strategies that did work. What did you notice?
I'm not sure I can do any of these.	If you could start one thing that would make a difference in the next month, what would that be?
I don't have time to do this.	Is this still important to you? What's the minimum length of time you need to get started?
I'm not sure I can follow through on this.	Let's assume you did follow through. How would things be better for you?

In the context of a learning conversation (typically a far less intimidating exchange than a job interview), an appropriate response might be a paraphrase that opens with frames like "What we seem to be talking about is…" or "It sounds like…." With that said, paraphrasing can be helpful even when your conversation partner doesn't explicitly ask you for such feedback. An example follows:

Conversation partner: *I'm struggling with competing priorities at the moment and don't feel like I'm doing any of them justice. It's just been so busy. I feel like I bounce from one meeting to another and then don't get time to do the actual work emerging from the meetings. I need to get some clear headspace to progress my own work, too.*

Conversation leader: *It sounds like there's a lot going on for you right now, and this seems to be impacting your sense of progress and "doing things justice." It sounds like there is an issue around the number of priorities, meetings, and lack of space between them that's limiting your headspace to get the work done.*

As we mentioned in the listening section, whenever possible, we recommend including your partner's own words within your paraphrase. Sometimes we refer to this as "parrot-phrasing;" however, again, we stress that you need not play back a precise transcript of every word. Instead, as in the example above, aim to select and emphasize the most resonant words and phrases, such as "doing any of them justice," making "progress," and "headspace"—words that capture the essence of the partner's predicament.

Sometimes our partner describes their situation metaphorically. Metaphors are particularly powerful tools in coaching (provided that they originate with the coachee) since they often use potent imagery and convey a deeper meaning than a more literal statement. Let's say that your conversation partner in the example above informs you that "the pot is boiling over," a metaphor signifying that their world is "out of control." You can then use their metaphor to hint at their desired future and possible actions by using language like "So you want to bring the pot back down to a simmer?" or "What are some things that could help get a lid on the pot" or "How might you turn the heat down?"

SUMMARIZING

As with paraphrasing, summarizing demonstrates that we are listening attentively and serves to clarify what has been said. When our partner is in an exploratory thinking-aloud mode with multiple components, we might use a lengthy paraphrase to help them clarify their thinking. But in other situations, a summary uses fewer words to get to the heart of the matter and generate momentum in a conversation. Summarizing (using fewer words) is also a good way to follow up and can serve as a quick check on the accuracy of what we think we are hearing as the conversation leader.

Summarizing statements in response to the example earlier could be:

Conversation partner: *I'm struggling with competing priorities at the moment and don't feel like I'm doing any of them justice. It's just been so busy. I feel like I bounce from one meeting to another and then don't get time to do the actual work emerging from the meetings. I need to get some clear headspace to progress my own work too.*

Conversation leader: *It sounds like you want to be able to manage those competing priorities so that you have more headspace to do quality work. Have I got that right?*

Or

Conversation leader: *It sounds like there are two related things at play here—the competing priorities and the way in which meetings eat up your time. Would that be fair to say?*

Or

Conversation leader: *Ah, headspace to progress your own work? Tell me more about that.*

This last response is a so-called *bridging question* that serves as an invitation to expand on a key phrase or term. Even in the absence of the "tell me more" prompt, our conversation partner might very well continue talking (and, therefore, thinking) when presented with the single-word summary statement, "Headspace?..."

Earlier in this chapter, we stressed the importance of listening for emotions. Here, we introduce the term *emotional paraphrase*, a short-form appraisal of the underlying emotions beneath the actual words of your partner. We may not always read every emotional subtext with accuracy; however, even if we are slightly off the mark, the practice can still be helpful, as in the example below.

Conversation partner: *We had a team meeting yesterday, and I thought we had an honest and robust conversation about the recent assessment data. I thought I led* *the discussion well and that I gave everyone a voice in the discussion. Even David seemed to contribute constructively, and I thought we'd reached consensus. But I was apparently wrong about that. I just heard this morning that he went over my head to the assistant principal to complain about what was agreed to in the course of the meeting.*

Conversation leader [reading the tone and body language]: *It sounds like you're quite angry about that?*

Conversation partner: *Hmm, no, I don't think it's anger. I'm just really disappointed.*

PARAPHRASING AND SUMMARIZING BY LISTING, ORGANIZING, AND PRIORITIZING

In the prior example about competing priorities, the conversation partner engages in a think-aloud in which they allude to multiple factors that have contributed to their problem. A skilled conversation leader can help their partner organize and prioritize their thinking simply by teasing out and listing the most important threads or themes at different stages of the conversation. For example, at the start of the conversation (the think-aloud), we might respond to our partner's problem statement by listing each contributing factor to direct the conversation toward what seems the most important area of focus:

You seem to be grappling with several things here:

- Lots of competing priorities right now.
- Being involved in a high number of meetings.
- Finding the time and headspace to progress your own priorities.

In this case, when we play back each factor in the form of a concise bulleted list, our conversation partner can identify what is most important in the context of the conversation and prioritize the items according to levels of importance or urgency.

We can also employ listing at other stages of the conversation such as the Options and Tactics stages. After the partner engages in divergent thinking and names various options they might pursue, the conversation leader can list these options and invite their partner to select the best possibilities from the list. Similarly, at the Tactics stage, where we get specific about how we will make progress, the conversation leader narrows down and lists each step (e.g., when, how, with whom) from the partner's thinking to help them articulate these in precise language. The leader can also confirm whether these steps are in the correct sequence and invite comment on what might be missing. At this point, it can be very helpful for the conversation partner to write down the steps.

In a recent conversation with one of our esteemed colleagues at GCI, Lucy Carroll, she described paraphrasing and summarizing as the "sleeper skills" of coaching and stated that if she had to rank-order each skill, she would place them higher than questioning. We agree. In our experience working with novice coaches and leaders, these powerful skills are frequently underutilized. While you may be tempted to bombard your conversation partner with one question after another, many times you can better support their thinking by simply restating what you "think they told you" by using well-crafted and well-timed paraphrases or summary statements.

SHARING KNOWLEDGE AND PERSPECTIVE

To some in the coaching world, the inclusion of this skill may seem at odds with the philosophy of pure (entirely facilitative) coaching. Although this book relates primarily to contexts apart from formal coaching and takes a broader view, we respect the facilitative origins of coaching and acknowledge that the inclusion of this skill comes with some qualifications. First, effective conversation leaders know when and how to share their knowledge or perspective in the interest of helping their conversation partners think more clearly and make progress. The ability to do this clearly and sensitively is a skill that is fundamental to the dialogical stance. Experienced instructional coaches and mentors know that possessing knowledge, expertise, and experience is not sufficient—they also need to be effective explainers and modelers and appreciate the fact that simply telling and showing does not generally effect sustained change in the teacher with whom they are working. Since most of us are "helpful advice givers" (we might even say "serial advice givers"), aspiring coaches and conversation leaders need to become consciously aware of this tendency and learn to regulate it. You can begin by working to understand where this default behavior comes from and, more importantly, how to manage it. Default doesn't mean fixed or immutable, and we can learn to self-regulate. Moreover, within schools and other organizations, such behavior often has a socially constructed component.

The influential organizational psychologist Edgar Schein (2009) suggested that anyone in a perceived helper role automatically is cast as the more powerful person in the conversation. When such helpers are also formal leaders or supervise their conversation partner, they assume even greater power. Conversely, those who seek help default to a position that Schein calls "one downness" (p. 31). As mentioned in our prior discussion of listening with humility, conversation leaders can also intentionally place themselves in a position of one downness by taking the role of learner in the conversation and dialing down their tendency to share knowledge and give advice.

The perils and pitfalls of our advice-giving tendencies featured prominently in Michael Bungay Stanier's hugely popular and successful book *The Coaching Habit* (2016), so much so that the sequel, *The Advice Trap* (2020), is devoted entirely to the topic. Stanier sums up the challenge in graphic terms:

> *It turns out that being more coach-like and staying curious a little longer is harder than most of us thought. No matter our good intentions, we love to give advice. We love it. As soon as someone starts talking, our plan to be curious goes out the door and our Advice Monster looms out of our subconscious, rubbing its hands and declaring, "I'm about to add some value to this conversation! Yes. I. Am!"* (2020, p. 3)

So, what can we do to manage our tendency to give advice or offer suggestions, too soon and too frequently? Leading proponent of solutions-focused coaching, Mark McKergow (2009), proposed a "spectrum of places where know-how might emerge" (p. 52) and, as we have already discussed, highlighted one of the most common questions asked by people learning to be more coach-like in conversations—when and how can I use my knowledge and expertise?

The Know-How Continuum depicted in Figure 6.3 is our adaptation of McKergow's spectrum of places. It includes examples of questions that leaders can use to bring their partners closer to solutions. These questions fall under three sources of know-how, starting with the conversation partner and moving to what the conversation leader brings to the conversation. We use these questions to support our conversation partner in accessing know-how from the various sources with the goal of generating multiple options (the O in our GROWTH framework). As illustrated, we find it helpful to imagine a metaphorical pool of options that we are trying to populate with a range of possibilities.

FIGURE 6.3
The Know-How Continuum

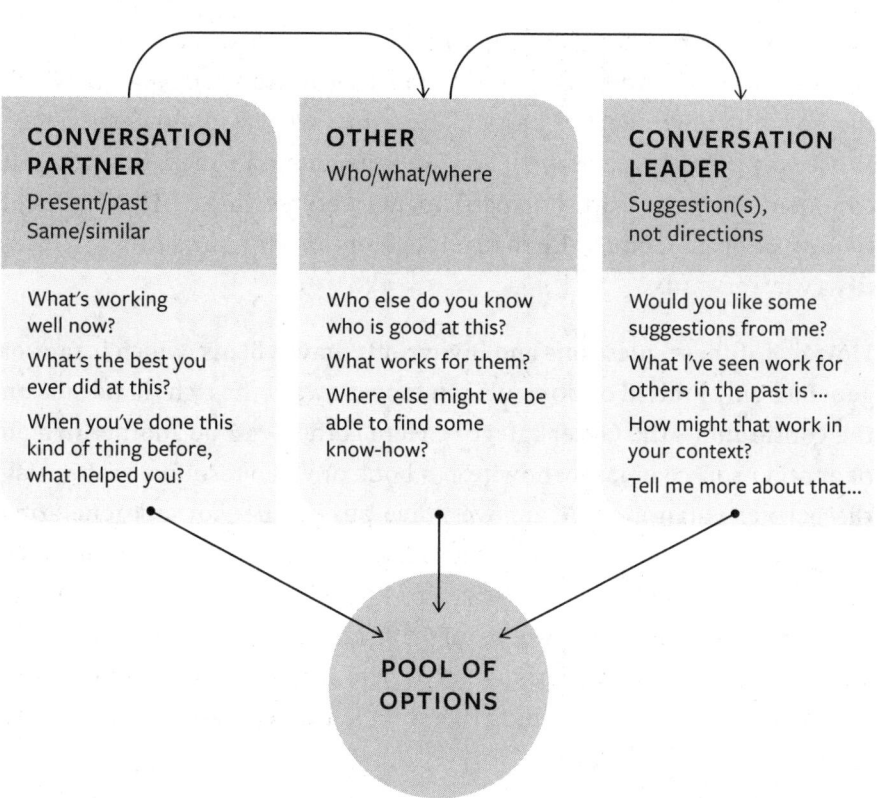

When we adopt a facilitative stance in the conversation, we zero in on what our conversation partner brings to the table at present, from the past, and from those around them and their environment—in other words, the first two sources of know-how on the continuum. Ideally, we want our conversation partner to rely on their own resources and serve as their own primary source of know-how. We can guide them to a greater sense of self-reliance by asking questions that focus their attention on what might help them now as well as asking them to reflect on what has worked for them in the past when faced with similar challenges. Helpful questions can be as simple as "What's working well now?" or "What is already in place that could help here?" We might also invite our partner to think about the same or similar situations in the past. Questions like "When you've done this kind of thing before, what helped you?" or an invitation like "Tell me about a time in the past when you've effectively overcome a similar challenge" can surface strategies that the conversation partner had forgotten over time.

Skilled conversation leaders pose questions and offer invitations that lead their conversation partners to consider positive counternarratives to their current challenge as a way to advance themselves toward future possibilities, such as "When has there been a time when your students were just a bit more engaged?" or "Tell me about a meeting you ran in the past in which there was a higher level of participation than what you now experience. What was the difference then?" or "Tell me about a time when you felt confident that your workshop participants were 'getting it.' These lines of inquiry often generate more than enough options for our partner to identify a way forward.

However, if these questions and invitations draw a blank, which is rare, or generate only limited options, we can move toward the right-hand side on the continuum—the Other category. Here, "other" can be another person or another source of know-how (e.g., a book or video resource with which the partner is familiar). Again, we guide our partner toward generating their own options by using an invitational rather than directive tone. Key questions here include "Who else do you know who does this well?" "What works for them?" and "Where else might you find more information to help you formulate different options…?" When our partners start to believe that they can find the solutions to their problems themselves, they are more empowered to take action.

By now, our partners most likely have several possibilities bobbing around in the pool of options, and we sense they may be sufficient to facilitate progress. However, this is not always the case. Conversation leaders must be prepared to support their partners when they feel stuck. This can occur early in their trajectory toward goal attainment or at any point in the process. The partner either cannot envision options or has never encountered a similar challenge in the past. They may signal their "stuckness" in plain language (e.g., "I don't know. What do you think?"). At such times, remind yourself that such impasses are not a negative reflection on your coaching expertise. It is an indication that you have held a facilitative stance long enough and need to move to a dialogical stance. Still controlling your urge to give direct advice, and guided by internal mantras like "Tell less, ask more," you are now ready to share some of your knowledge or perspective. When we are faithfully adopting a dialogical stance, we consciously avoid the trap of asking leading questions that are, in actuality, thinly disguised pieces of advice (e.g., "Have you thought of…?" or "Do you think you could…?").

Such leading questions are tell-tale examples of what Michael Bungay Stanier (2016) calls "offering up advice with a question mark attached" (p. 75).

Having exhausted every facilitative possibility, you can now move to the right-hand side of the continuum and the final source of know-how—what *you* bring to the table as the conversation leader. But first, we need to offer some important caveats that will help keep your conversation partner in the driver's seat:

1. When we offer suggestions, however well intentioned, we do so through our own contextual lens. This can never be the same as someone else's lens. Our lens is based on our own life experience, beliefs, assumptions, and so on. For this reason, we need to (tactfully) present possibilities in the form of our suggestions.

2. A dialogical stance involves sharing suggestions rather than giving advice. Giving advice is directive and leaves much less room for adaptation and choice than offering suggestions. Use of the words "you should" or, worse yet, "you must" is ill advised in that they signify directions rather than suggestions.

3. Suggesting means adding options to the pool. We are not advocating for our way.

4. The language we use is provisional and tentative. This avoids putting our partner in the position of having to agree or disagree with our suggestions.

5. These approaches convey humility and prioritize the voice and choice of our partner.

In the spirit of being provisional, our opening question might be "Would you like some suggestions from me?" While most of the time this will be met with a resounding "Yes, please!" there are exceptions. Be prepared for times when your partner signals that your change in stance is premature and that they are still thinking things through. Even when your partner invites you to share your expertise or knowledge, resist the seductive draw of advice giving (Schein, 2009) and the temptation to overplay your contribution. Our default rule is still "Less is more." The example that follows depicts a sequence in which the leader provides "just enough" input, using provisional language to enable their partner to begin to grasp a possibility and relate it to their own context.

- **Would you like some suggestions from me?** Always begin by seeking permission. Also note the use of the plural *suggestions*. Ideally, we want to be able to offer several options to enable choice.

- **What I've seen work for others in the past is…or…What's worked for me in similar situations is.…** Notice that this option comes from experience with others and is stated as something that worked in the past. In the second version, the word *similar* underscores that the leader's world is not the same as the partner's. The phrasing of both statements makes each suggestion less personal and, therefore, easier for the partner to reject.

- **How might those options work in your context?** Note the use of provisional language: *options* (i.e., optional) and *might* (i.e., not certain). This question is inviting our partner to engage with our suggestions as they relate to their world—their situation and context. At this point, we are in a dialogical stance so that we can both consider the options together.

- **Tell me more about that.** If our partner sees one of our options as feasible, even just an aspect of it, this invitation moves the conversation leader into a facilitative stance as our partner fully takes the wheel by beginning to shape the option and make it their own.

EXCEPTIONS: WHEN ADVICE IS WHAT'S NEEDED

Of course, there are times when going straight to advice is what is required and expected. Equally, we don't always have the luxury of time in schools, and we are likely to encounter scenarios in which taking a facilitative stance could easily backfire. For example, if a beginning teacher is really struggling in a completely unfamiliar situation and is on the verge of leaving the profession, the first thing they might need is a metaphorical life jacket rather than a question that comes from a place of curiosity. Once their world is stabilized and their head is above water again, we might then start to build from their resources. Similarly, teachers encounter such crisis scenarios with great frequency in their relationships with students and generally can discern when a directive stance is warranted.

Chris experienced a less extreme example of this in a recent exchange with his colleague, Jon (not his real name). Our organization introduced a new online coaching log, and Chris forgot how to log into the system. He phoned Jon, our administrative assistant, for quick advice on how to proceed. Jon, who had just completed a coaching course, still had the "Ask, don't tell" mantra in his head when he received the distress call from Chris.

Here's how the conversation went:

Chris: Sorry to be a pest, Jon, but I've forgotten how to log in and record my coaching sessions. I have a bit of a backlog, and the end of the month is tomorrow.

Jon: Oh, OK then, when has there been a time in the past when you have been successful at this?

Chris: When we did it in the training session a couple of months ago.

Jon: So what could you do to make progress on this?

Chris [slightly frustrated]: I'm doing it, I've called you for help.

Jon: Great, and what else could you do?

Chris: Um, I really just need you to show me how to do it properly so that I can get the sessions entered before the end of the month.

In this exchange, Jon tried to avoid giving advice and instead attempted to take a facilitative stance in what was meant to be a transactional exchange. Chris, on the other hand, was pressed for time and made it clear from the outset that what he needed was advice. Moreover, the advice that Chris needed was technical and straightforward, and his "problem" only had a single solution: He needed to be reminded of how to log onto the system. They both knew that Jon was the holder of the knowledge that Chris needed. Having said this, if, after receiving explicit log-in instructions from Jon, Chris still hasn't learned (or remembered) the procedure a month later and, again, turns to Jon for help, a dialogical stance may be warranted. In response to Chris's second appeal, Jon might then suggest that they work to identify ways to reinforce Chris's procedural knowledge so that it finally sticks.

The skills of noticing and discerning are key to knowing when and how to deploy our knowledge, expertise, or perspective in conversations. Even when our partner asks us to make suggestions, we don't direct or position ourselves as the expert in the room. Rather, we maintain our curiosity and engage in what Schein (2009) calls "humble inquiry" (p. 66). Similarly, as Bungay-Stanier (2020) puts it, "we rest our overdeveloped advice-giving muscle a bit whilst working on developing an underused muscle—curiosity" (p. 65).

NOTICING

Van Nieuwerburgh (2020) defines the skill of noticing in coaching as "becoming conscious of information that may be useful to coachees and the coaching process" (p. 65) and calls it an essential coaching skill. We can all get better at noticing, a skill that helps us make better decisions as conversation leaders.

As we've discussed throughout this chapter, conversation leaders can choose from a wide variety of "next moves" in response to what they have heard from their conversation partner. Noticing involves being attuned to cues in the conversation that help us determine our next coaching (or leading) move. For example, we may notice important words or phrases that are worth playing back in the form of a paraphrase or summary. As we listen for and notice these cues, we are likely to ask ourselves questions about the choices we make that will support our partner's progress, such as the following:

- What type of question might be most helpful right now?
- Do they need more thinking time, (in which case, I'll stay quiet)?
- Should I express empathy, or should I just attempt to reframe the conversation?
- Should I ask them about possible resources?
- Is this an opportunity to affirm a strength or skill?
- Have I exhausted all possibilities, and is it now time to ask permission to share knowledge?

In some ways, noticing is a skill that influences how we use the other coaching skills. The more we master the skill, the more discerning we are about taking a particular stance or determining an appropriate conversational context. Some additional internal questions that relate to various points on the Learning Conversations Map include the following:

- How do I need to "be" (i.e., what stance do I take) in this conversation based on what I am noticing about my conversation partner?
- What do I notice about the context of the conversation, and do I need to manage the space in a particular way?

- What do I notice about how my partner is presenting right now, and what do I need to be mindful of in how I respond? (Again, this relates to stance, which we can adjust depending on our partner's responses.)
- What am I noticing about myself as the conversation unfolds; for example, is my Advice Monster (Stanier, 2020) climbing onto my shoulder, and how will I manage this? (On the Learning Conversations Map, this tendency to advise takes us toward the most direct end of the axis.)

Adapting the work of van Nieuwerburgh (2020), Figure 6.4 offers some suggestions of things that we can notice about our conversation partner, ourselves, and the context of the conversation to help us discern our next move.

FIGURE 6.4
Things We Can Helpfully Notice

Things We Might Notice in Our Partners	Things We Might Notice in Ourselves	Things We Might Notice About the Context of the Conversation
Readiness	Readiness	Physical environment
Energy	Energy	Time available
Openness to challenge	Presence	Passing of time
Body language	Availability	Other people
Choice of language	Advice-giving tendency	Distractions
Emotional state	Your thinking	Notetaking
Resourcefulness	Emotional triggers	Privacy
Their thinking patterns	Who they remind you of	
Patterns of behavior	What their issue reminds you of	
Self-limiting beliefs or actions	Tone	
Assumptions	Body language	
Strengths	Expression	

Source: Adapted from information in C. van Nieuwerburgh, *An Introduction to Coaching Skills: A Practical Guide* (3rd edition), 2020.

More fundamentally, noticing is central to self-awareness and awareness of others. Daniel Goleman (1995), one of the leading experts in the field of emotional intelligence, reminds us that these two qualities help us to manage ourselves and maintain positive relationships with others. We will say more about this in the next chapter when we explore a coaching way of being.

THE SUBTLETIES OF LANGUAGE IN SUPPORTING THINKING AND PROGRESS

In the life of schools, we use language and words with such regularity that we rarely get to question their purpose in communication. For many years, the predominant belief was that words and questions are merely tools that convey an objective reality. In the context of clinical psychology, for example, a therapist might interview a client by posing questions that revealed the client's innermost thoughts and feelings. Other disciplines and professions subscribed to similar beliefs about the purpose of questions. As professionals, we use questions to help ourselves and others to perform our jobs more effectively. For example, a teacher may pose questions to their students to better gauge the extent of their learning. Doctors question their patients to understand their symptoms and consequently diagnose and treat them. Likewise, in our more casual, interpersonal interactions, we listen and question others to understand where they are coming from and how to respond appropriately.

In recent times, social constructionist theories have argued that the words we use actually shape the interactions and the meaning that both conversation partners take from the interaction. This is an important shift. For example, David Cooperrider, a pioneer in appreciative inquiry—a strengths-based approach to organizational change—has argued that "We live in worlds our conversations create" (as cited in Stavros & Torres, 2019, p. 1). Similarly, Jackie Kelm, in *Appreciative Living* (2005), argues that "Words create worlds" (p. 26). Corporate lawyer Justin Whitmel Earley makes a similar claim in the context of a specific type of work. When asked about his occupation, Earley responds, "I change things through words." He maintains that, as a mergers and acquisitions lawyer, he uses words to create agreements between people and organizations, thus bringing into being things that had not existed before. "One moment there was no merger, and the next there is, simply because of words. Words create new realities" (Earley, 2019, p. 32). In many ways, those working as both leaders and coaches are doing something similar: They help people change things through words.

Our purpose in discussing these differing perspectives on language, words, and questions is to underscore that, as conversation leaders, our words matter. When we choose our words with intentionality, we can help our conversation partners shape their reality by moving beyond their problems to solutions. For example, when we pose a question beginning with the stem "why," the most we can accomplish is to further our partner's understanding of the root causes of their problem. However, understanding causality is not generally sufficient to move them closer to finding solutions. In fact, asking "why?" in relation to complex challenges is more likely to take the conversation down less helpful, and more time-consuming, avenues.

Asking "why?" is useful in a conversation that seeks to get to a root cause in a thing-related problem (e.g., why the internet has suddenly stopped working is worth discovering so that we can go to the root cause to fix the problem); however, it doesn't seem to be such a useful question in people-related problems. Solution-focused approaches suggest that in people-related challenges, gaining a detailed understanding of a root cause does not necessarily help get closer to solutions. As Evan George, Chris Iveson, and Harvey Ratner (2013) have stated in their work on solutions-focused therapy, "attempting to understand the cause of a problem is not a necessary or particularly useful step toward resolution" (p. 27).

Coaches and leaders who apply a solutions-focused approach intentionally choose words that stimulate progress toward a more desirable future. Consider the impact of shifting your language in response to problem-focused statements from "Why did this happen?" to "What would you like to see happen instead of what you just described?" This simple but powerful shift in language moves the conversation (and our partner) from being stuck in a problematic present to the possibility of a brighter future. The most effective conversation leaders notice the subtleties of language and can skillfully initiate language shifts to help their partners do their best thinking.

PUTTING IT INTO PRACTICE

The Key Skills Checklist in Figure 6.5 describes the characteristics of the five skills we have outlined in this chapter. In addition to a helpful summary, we recommend that you use the checklist as a reflection tool as you develop your skills as a conversation leader. It can be helpful to return to the checklist periodically to gauge the progress you have made.

FIGURE 6.5
Key Skills Checklist

This checklist describes the characteristics of five key skills of an effective conversation leader. We invite you to rate yourself on a scale of 1–5, where 1 means you do it poorly and 5 means you do it well, for each key skill.

	1	2	3	4	5
1. Listening to Encourage Thinking • I listen at least twice as much as I speak. • I refrain from interrupting. • I wait until someone has completely finished speaking before sharing my thoughts. • I avoid completing people's sentences. • I maintain appropriate eye contact and open body language in conversations. • I use encouraging nods and minimal prompts to let others know I am listening. • I can comfortably manage silence in a conversation without trying to fill it.					
2. Asking Powerful Questions • I ask open-ended questions that invite deeper thinking. • I ask only one question at a time, allowing people to reflect and answer. • I avoid giving advice through leading questions such as "Have you tried…?" • I begin my questions with open starters such as how, what, where, and who. • I ask questions that demonstrate curiosity. • I ask thought-provoking questions. • I ask questions that seek commitment. • I ask solution-focused questions that focus on desired results.					
3. Summarizing and Paraphrasing • I summarize what I hear into fewer words. • I refocus the attention of the conversation through summarizing and paraphrasing.					

	1	2	3	4	5
3. Summarizing and Paraphrasing—(continued) • I use summarizing to reframe the other person's perception of a situation. • I use paraphrasing to reflect back what the other person has said. • I include some of the other person's language when summarizing. • I use paraphrasing and summarizing to confirm that there is shared understanding.					
4. Noticing • I am aware of my own body language and the body language of the other person. • I am aware of my own emotions and the emotions of the other person. • I notice how others are reacting through verbal and nonverbal cues. • I notice my own energy levels and that of others in a conversation. • I notice my own tendency to be either directive or nondirective. • I notice signals and words that provide information about a person's readiness. • I notice the environment around me when I have conversations.					
5. Sharing Knowledge and Perspective • I am careful to discern the usefulness of any contribution I might make before speaking. • I am cautious and intentional about what, when, and how I contribute. • I ask permission before offering my perspective or suggestions. • When sharing my knowledge or perspective, I use provisional language. • I invite the other person to consider and contextualize my suggestions or perspective. • I seek to allow my conversation partner choice.					

CHAPTER 7

Showing Up in Conversations: A Coaching Way of Being

> *"Very small change starts from very small conversations, held among people who care."*
> **MARGARET WHEATLEY (2002)**

In Chapter 3, we introduced the concept of stance and defined it as a combination of how we consciously show up and what we do to support the thinking and progress of our conversation partner. Our Learning Conversations Map (Chapter 4) included a horizontal axis depicting the degrees of our management and contribution as the conversation leader. The what-we-do part of stance is about utilizing the coaching frameworks, skills, and techniques, which we covered in Chapters 5 and 6.

How we show up as the conversation leader is the final, and possibly most critical, element of bringing a coaching approach to our leadership. It's more than what we do—the ways that we lead and manage the conversation. It is about how we are or, more specifically, how our conversation partner perceives and experiences us in the conversation. In formal coaching contexts, we could describe this as the difference between doing coaching and being a coach.

A COACHING WAY OF BEING

The concept of a coaching way of being has been defined and elaborated upon by Christian van Nieuwerburgh in the third edition of *An Introduction to Coaching Skills* (2020). Recognizing the somewhat fuzzy nature of this concept, van Nieuwerburgh describes the development of a coaching way of being as an ongoing journey and suggests that it is not learned and developed in the same way as skills and other techniques. Unlike a discrete technical skill that can be demonstrated and practiced, learning how to show up for others will not happen in an hour-long workshop or by watching a YouTube video. However, we believe that with conscious effort, noticing, and reflection we can all develop and sustain new and more helpful ways of showing up for others.

To make this concept more concrete and tangible, van Nieuwerburgh describes the ideal attributes of a coach as humility, confidence, empathy, belief in others, respect, integrity, and intercultural sensitivity (which we reframe later in this chapter).

You may recall that some of these same attributes match those presented when we talked about listening skills. In this chapter, we encourage you to think beyond skills and to consider these attributes as uniquely human characteristics that we embody. We believe that a coaching way of being is a default component of a coaching approach. We do not choose to be less humble, respectful, or empathetic at different points in our conversations. Our coaching way of being should remain intact, even as we shift stance in the conversation. For example, offering some of our knowledge or expertise does not mean we cease to be respectful and empathetic to our partner. As we've emphasized, after first asking permission to share, we respectfully propose some suggestions to add to the pool of options (Figure 6.2). How we do this—our tone, our choice of language, our demeanor—will largely determine how our partner experiences us and, in turn, how they feel and respond. Our beliefs about our fellow educators, ourselves, our roles, and the functioning of our organizations have an impact on how (or if) these attributes manifest. For example, if we assume that a teacher (or member of our leadership team) has the capacity to think, learn, grow, and innovate, our confidence and belief in them will come through in our conversations with them.

In his seminal text *Unmistakable Impact* (2011), Jim Knight proposed a set of partnership principles that ground the way effective instructional coaches interact with teachers. In a later work, *The Definitive Guide to Instructional Coaching* (2022), Knight summarizes these enduring principles as "a way of being for mutually humanizing conversation" (p. 16).

The following list contains Knight's seven partnership principles as applied to leaders of learning conversations:

- **Equality:** I believe that my conversation partner, and their contributions, are as valuable as my own.
- **Choice:** I believe that my conversation partner should have choice and that this lies at the heart of autonomy and agency as a thinking professional.
- **Voice:** I consciously privilege, elevate, and amplify the thoughts, ideas, emotions, and contextual understanding of my conversation partner.
- **Reflection:** I view my conversation partner as a thinking professional, and my role is to respectfully support them to reflect critically on situations in order to enable insight and progress.
- **Dialogue:** I seek to engage my conversation partner in a sense-making conversation where we think together and shape each other's ideas.
- **Praxis:** I understand that the learning of my conversation partner is applied through action and reflection in their real-world context.
- **Reciprocity:** I approach learning conversations expecting to learn with and from my partner.

Synthesizing the work of van Nieuwerburgh (2020) and Knight (2011, 2022), we propose the following as characteristics of how effective conversation leaders show up for their conversation partners: humility and respect; belief in others, care, and empathy; integrity; cultural capability; confidence; and a solution-focused orientation.

HUMILITY AND RESPECT

We demonstrate humility by setting aside our expertise, knowledge, and perspective until it is absolutely needed. It may seem paradoxical, but we bring expertise without showing up as the expert. We are respectfully curious and aim to keep our conversation partner in the driver's seat by seeking to privilege and amplify their voice and choice in the conversation.

In the influential book, *Humble Inquiry: The Gentle Art of Asking Instead of Telling*, organizational psychologist Edgar Schein (Schein & Schein, 2021) introduced the concept of here-and-now humility:

> *Here-and-now humility is how you feel when you realize that you are dependent on someone else in the situation. Your status is inferior to*

> *the other person at that moment because he or she knows something or can do something that you need in order to accomplish your task or goal. (p. 22)*

While Schein initially focused on a hierarchical relationship in which leaders depend upon subordinates for their expertise and skills, which, in turn, enable the leaders to realize their own (or an organization's) goals, we find the concept of dependency applicable to the broader context of conversation leaders and partners. Regardless of your (and your partner's) hierarchical positions, when you lead with humility, you place yourself in a position of dependency, at least in the context of the conversation. As we stressed in the preceding chapter, your conversation partner is invariably the expert on their own perceived reality.

Schein links this form of humility to curiosity:

> *My here-and-now humility can by itself trigger a very positive and genuine curiosity and interest in you. You will feel acknowledged, and it is precisely my temporary "subordination" that can create psychological safety for you. (p. 26)*

Educators may find it challenging to assume this "subordinate" role in a learning conversation, even knowing full well that the arrangement is temporary by design. Teachers are accustomed to a power dynamic in which their students depend on them as their teacher and as the "adult in the room." We can get beyond our initial discomfort with handing over the wheel when we remind ourselves that our purpose in doing so is to support our partner's thinking and help them achieve a more positive future for themselves and, ultimately, their students.

In much the same way, the conversation leader listens attentively to understand and, more important, to help their conversation partner understand. We do so by noticing and suspending our judgments, assumptions, and conclusions, even if we are certain we have the answer. In doing so, we give our partner the opportunity to think aloud and reach their own conclusions. But when we conclude that shifting to a dialogical stance is appropriate (ideally, when our partner signals that they are ready for it), we exhibit humility by offering our perspective and suggestions in an emotionally intelligent and respectful manner. We use the tentative language presented in Chapter 6 to test our assumption that our partner is ready for more input from us, and we actively build on what they contribute. Here we and our partners are experiencing Knight's (2011) partnership principles of equality, voice, choice, dialogue, and reciprocity.

BELIEF IN OTHERS, CARE, AND EMPATHY

As conversation leaders, we need to have faith in our conversation partner's capacity to learn, grow, and realize their goals. For a teacher, this belief is akin to having a growth mindset and holding high expectations for our students. When we believe in our conversation partner's potential for growth and success, we are less likely to default to a directive stance. A facilitative or dialogical stance, therefore, evokes more genuine engagement and thinking. Conversely, if our expectations are low, we are more likely to cut to the chase by offering unsolicited advice or asking leading questions. Moreover, such "advice" is often suspect because it is informed by our own beliefs, biases, and experiences.

We show empathy by taking the time to listen without judgment and seeking to clarify how they experience their current reality. We also listen beneath the surface by noticing and naming underlying emotions that may not always be evident in their words but show up in their body language, tone of voice, or other nonverbal forms of expression. As we mentioned in the previous chapter, an expression of empathy is like an emotional paraphrase. That is, when we name the emotion accurately, our partner feels seen, and we build a stronger connection with them. If we get it slightly wrong, our partner will correct us and name the emotion themselves.

INTEGRITY

When conversation leaders display integrity, they build trust in their partners. We demonstrate integrity in a number of ways, beginning with listening attentively. Discretion is another component of integrity; for example, we explicitly discuss our commitment to keeping the conversation confidential, but we are also upfront about possible exceptions to this rule. Reliability also builds trust. We show this by consistently delivering on any promises we make ("Here is the email I promised") or just showing up on time. These often simple acts not only enhance our partner's levels of trust and psychological safety but also increase their levels of self-disclosure and candor.

CULTURAL CAPABILITY

Our cultural understandings influence how we perceive and experience our reality. Therefore, we can't check our culture at the door when we enter the school building. The same holds true for how we show up in conversations.

The influential psychologist Derald Wing Sue and colleagues have written extensively on the concept of "cultural competence" (Sue et al., 2022) in the field of counseling. They propose a multi-dimensional model that includes the awareness, knowledge, and skills required to form successful cross-cultural helping relationships. They emphasize that developing cultural competence is a lifelong process and that we must be continually mindful of how our own experiences, values, and biases affect our perceptions of and interactions with others.

Cultural capability is more than knowing about, and even valuing, another person's culture (Knight & Hill, 2023). We might go so far as to state that self-knowledge is every bit as important as our knowledge of our coachees and conversation partners. This is especially true when our partners don't share our cultural norms, lived experiences, or identities. Moreover, some argue that having the sensitivity, skills, and knowledge to engage in cross-cultural interactions may be insufficient in supporting our partner's progress toward attaining their desired outcomes.

We see a clear congruence between cultural capability and a coaching way of leading in that cultural capability (and humility) stresses an appreciation for and affirmation of another person's reality rather than filtering that person's reality through our own lens. As an example, consider that those of us who were raised and live in the dominant culture are unlikely to have shared many of the common negative experiences of conversation partners with marginalized identities. Consequently, when you listen attentively to your partner and attempt to read the emotional subtext beneath their words, it is essential to be cognizant of the limitations of your own cultural lens and enter into the conversation with openness, curiosity, and the sincere desire to learn from them. This has been described as cultural humility, a component of cultural capability (Hook et al., 2013).

CONFIDENCE

The most effective conversation leaders are confident in their ability to manage conversations toward a positive outcome for their conversation partner. We display confidence in our calm demeanor and self-assurance when we use our coaching skills to manage the pace and direction of the conversation. When conversation leaders are confident, they have a high threshold for uncertainty. More specifically, they are comfortable with the uncertainty of how the conversation will unfold and can stay focused on noticing and responding in the moment. A word of caution, however: If leaders overplay their display of confidence, our partners may interpret it as arrogance or assertiveness, leading to an unhelpful and undermining power differential.

Unlike listening or questioning—discrete skills that can be learned and practiced—confidence is something we embody; there aren't rules or guidelines to help us determine how much is "too much," and we intentionally positioned this discussion under ways of being rather than in the preceding chapter on skills. If a way of being is an external manifestation of our internal beliefs and values (many of which are influenced by culture), then confidence as a conversation leader is based on a strong (internal) sense of self-efficacy, or one's internal belief in the capacity to achieve a goal. Self-efficacy in the form of confidence as a conversation leaders takes time and experience to build. However, this shouldn't stop you from using your conversational leadership skills and knowledge to support your partner's progress.

A SOLUTION-FOCUSED ORIENTATION

Our approach to coaching is unabashedly infused with solution-focused techniques (McKergow, 2021; Jackson & McKergow, 2007). We have already addressed how to nurture a solution-focused orientation in our discussion of reframing problem talk. These reframing moves serve to redirect a conversation partner to the possibility of a more desirable status quo and help them make progress by considering both their internal and external resources. We briefly returned to a solution-focused orientation in this chapter to underscore its importance to a coaching way of being. It takes the form of an enduring bias toward possibility and an unwavering belief in a partner's capacity to find a solution, meet their challenges, and transform their reality. Coaching conversations have the power to awaken their optimism by increasing their levels of hopefulness, motivation, and self-efficacy. This optimism, or sense of positive possibility, will ultimately empower them to take steps toward a far brighter future.

We have now presented three core elements of effective coaching: (a) the GROWTH Framework as a way of bringing shape to learning conversations, (b) key coaching skills as the fuel of conversations, and (c) a coaching way of being as a default component of how leaders show up in conversations. In the next chapter, we will explore how these elements can be applied as a coaching approach in less formal conversational contexts.

PUTTING IT INTO PRACTICE

As with the key skills, a coaching way of being can be developed over time. The challenge, as we have described, is that developing it is less technical and can seem less tangible than practicing a new skill. The way we are is far more difficult to describe than the things we do. With this in mind, we invite you to reflect on each of the characteristics of a coaching way of being by considering the following two questions:

- What does this characteristic look, sound, and feel like when I am consciously living it out as a conversation leader?
- What does this characteristic look, sound, and feel like to my conversation partner?

You can dig deeper into your reflection by asking these supplementary questions:

- What will I notice?
- What will my conversation partner notice?
- What will be the signs of this, for me and for my partner?

03

A Coaching Approach in Less Formal Contexts

Chapter 8. Other-Initiated Conversations: "Got a Minute?"

Chapter 9. Leader-Initiated Conversations : "Can We Chat?"

CHAPTER 8

OTHER-INITIATED CONVERSATIONS: "GOT A MINUTE?"

> *"Solutions emerge when thoughts are rearranged or expanded."*
> MARCIA REYNOLDS (2020)

As we've stressed throughout this book, traditional, autocratic ways of leading fall short in today's complex, interconnected systems—especially human-intensive systems. The good news is that humans are magnificent learners and, with appropriate training and opportunities for practice, we can learn to transform ourselves and our organizations to embody a coaching way of leading. As we progress in our learning, our coaching agility increases, and we become able to turn even the most spontaneous "got a minute?" exchanges into "coachable moments."

A key theme of this chapter is building agility—particularly in those shorter exchanges that are initiated by others. What is now known as *agile thinking* developed in the software industry but has spread beyond that context and now informs various ways of exploring organizational change (Breakspear, 2017). Agile thinking promotes a fast-moving, experimental approach to change and encourages an alternative to traditional linear change models. It emphasizes starting small, learning quickly from successes and failures, and shifting direction as circumstances change and people learn new insights. It is not hard to see how this mode of thinking relates to the shifting stances of conversation leaders in response to the thinking and progress of our conversation partners.

Just as great teachers can turn an unplanned occurrence in the classroom into a memorable teachable moment, agile school leaders can transform any number of brief daily interactions into coachable moments. You may think of them as interruptions (and sometimes they are). Perhaps it's the colleague who comes to your office for quick advice or the teacher who needs to talk about an emotionally charged situation they recently experienced. Rather than viewing such encounters as interruptions, maximize these untapped opportunities to respond in the moment and, thereby, support your partner's thinking and progress toward a desired outcome. These types of conversations live in the bottom-left quadrant of the Learning Conversations Map (Figure 8.1).

FIGURE 8.1
Other-Initiated Conversations

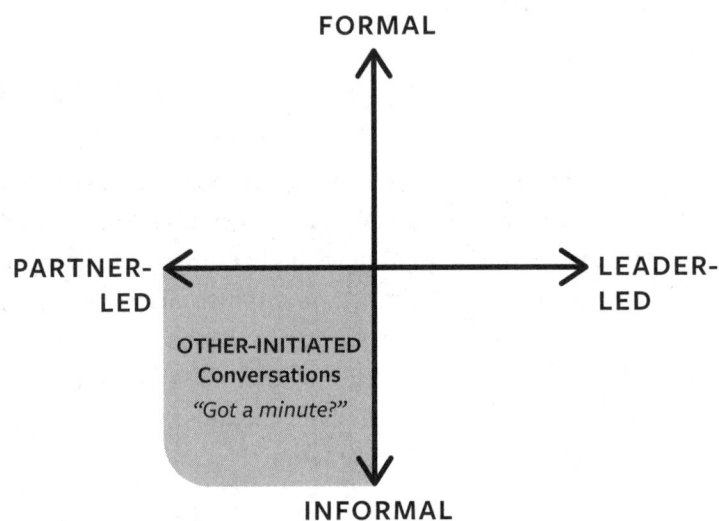

Sometimes it seems like our days are full of seemingly fragmented, hurried encounters, in which we are left with the feeling that we accomplished very little. And we are the first to acknowledge that there are times, such as when rushing to meet a pressing deadline or attending to a mounting crisis, when we are best served by rescheduling such conversations. However, we may be missing important opportunities to transform these encounters into coachable moments by applying a combination of intention, focus, and skill. This chapter will explore how these other-initiated, "got a minute?" conversations can be optimized in ways that benefit our colleagues, ourselves, and often the greater school community.

These learning conversations invoke the three elements of coaching (Campbell & van Nieuwerburgh, 2018; van Nieuwerburgh, 2020) that we discussed in greater depth in prior chapters: the conversational framework, the key skills of coaching, and a coaching way of being. However, in situations where we don't have the luxuries of time and/or an ideal setting, conversation leaders need to deploy these elements with great discernment and adaptability.

Let's now look at how this can be done.

DANCING AROUND THE GROWTH FRAMEWORK

In Chapter 5, we stressed that, although our presentation of the GROWTH framework (Figure 8.2) might suggest that its phases need to be rigidly sequenced and followed, GROWTH conversations are rarely that linear.

While there is some rationale for structuring a conversation in the sequence that appears in the graphic, more experienced conversation leaders make choices and use the framework flexibly and treat each letter as a guide rather than a strict pathway. Agility, in this context, means noticing where your conversation partner is at any given time and working with them to move through to the next most appropriate phase to help them make progress in the time available.

Let's take the example of a colleague who comes to you to discuss a complicated decision and already has some clarity on possible options. Your colleague has already engaged in the background thinking that typically takes place during the Goal and Reality phases; the conversation will commence in the Options (O) phase of the framework. In this "got a minute?" scenario, you aim to support your conversation partner by helping them

- **O (Options):** clarify their thinking about various options.
- **W (Will):** choose one or more specific options from the pool that will move them closer to their goals.
- **T (Tactics):** narrow down a course of action by considering how and when they will act on their intentions.
- **H (Habits):** when appropriate, think about how, after reaching their goal, they might sustain their success.

FIGURE 8.2
The GROWTH Framework

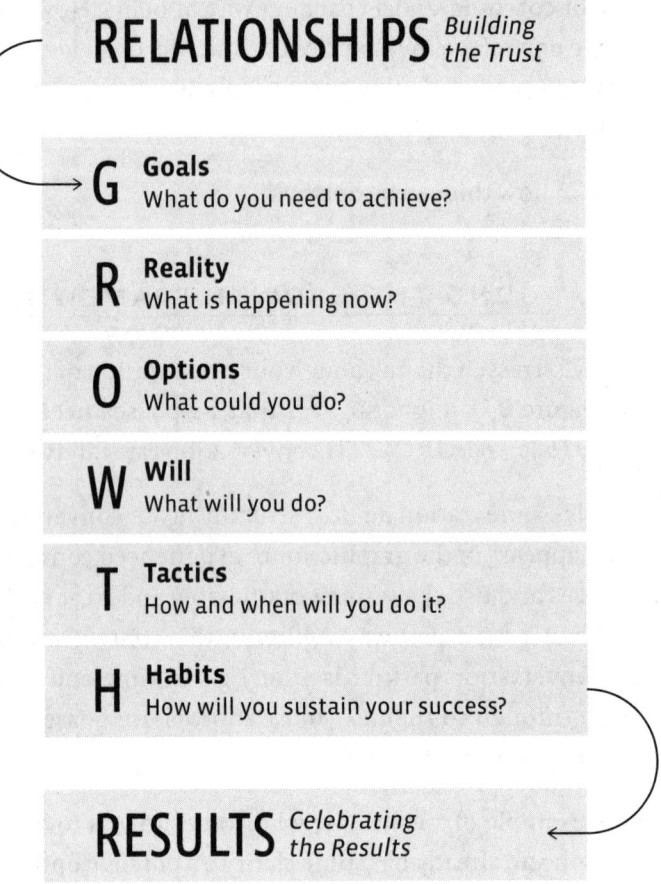

Source: From J. Campbell, 2016a. In C. van Nieuwerburgh (Ed.), *Coaching in Professional Contexts* (pp. 235–240). Used with permission.

Alternatively, you may discern that, rather than commencing the conversation with Options, you'll have a greater impact by gently guiding the conversation partner back to their original Goals (G) and inviting some clarification of the desired outcome. This course of action is especially useful if your partner articulates the options in the form of a binary (e.g., "Should I do this or that?"). They have narrowed down their options to two and are now feeling stuck because both options seem to have merit. In this instance, rather than cycling around the two options, you can help them reframe the binary question in a manner that more clearly connects the options to their desired outcome. Inviting your conversation partner to reframe the matter by changing the language and their question can open new thinking and progress. For example, instead of "Should I do this or that?," you can help them reframe the question to something like "What is the best option for…?" This new question can revisit the original purpose for the decision and may open up other alternatives to the binary "this or that" options currently being considered.

Another example of agile "dancing around GROWTH" may involve a colleague informally bringing up a particular problem they are experiencing. Typically, in such a situation, the colleague will describe what is not working and the negative emotions associated with the scenario and start at the Reality phase of GROWTH. An agile conversation leader notices this starting position and redirects the conversation back to the Goal phase by inviting their partner to describe what they would like to see instead of the deficit-based scenario they have just presented. The result of this conversation move is that they reframe their problem using affirmative, future-focused language. In doing so, they envision a positive alternative for themselves and their teammates and begin to feel more hopeful.

A GROWTH CONVERSATION IN 7 MINUTES

Rather than rigid adherence to a prescribed pathway, agile conversation leaders make flexible use of the GROWTH framework in response to their conversation partner's needs. "Got a minute?" conversations follow mini-loops across various stages that mirror the thinking of our conversation partners in response to our prompts.

To help build your agility as a leader, think about some recent in-the-moment interactions that you had with colleagues and how the use of the prompts below might have elevated the conversation in a way that furthered your partner's thinking and progress.

1. **What's most on your mind about this?** (Reality/Goal). This is frequently a helpful question to get to the essence of the topic being explored.

2. **So, what would you like to see happen here instead?** (Goal). A question of this type begins to shift the focus toward what's wanted and away from problem talk.

3. **And, what else would you be noticing if this situation was resolved… perfectly?** (Goal). The use of the word *noticing* helps to keep the description focused on specific observable characteristics of what's wanted.

4. **So, you'd be noticing...and...and...** (Goal). This is clearly not a question but a key point to offer a summary. Often, our conversation partner will take it as an invitation to add more—"Yes! And..."

5. **So that's where you would like to get to on this?** (Goal). We do not use closed questions very often in coaching conversations, but they can be helpful to bring focus and highlight a decision point, especially when used in in-the-moment conversations where time is short. Often this question serves as a prompt for moving to action.

6. **What's already happening that's helping you move in that direction?** (Resources). This question prompts our partner to identify resources within and around them and to acknowledge that there is usually some source of energy to fuel progress.

7. **And, what else? And, what else?** (Resources/Options). Sensitive probing for more detail via "And, what else?" frequently draws out more helpful details.

8. **So, what would be a sign you were just a little bit closer to that ideal resolution of this?** (Goal). Drawing attention to even small signs of progress helps to build a sense of possibility and motivation.

9. **And what's one small action you can take toward that sign in the next 24 hours?** (Tactics). Similarly, a focus on one small next step rather than a long list of action steps helps build confidence that progress is possible.

10. **Will you do that and let me know how you get on?** (Habits). This small check-in mechanism helps to generate commitment. It also emphasizes that progress is incremental and that you as the conversation leader are there as a source of supportive accountability.

CONDENSED GROWTH (G-R-T): THREE QUESTIONS TO GUIDE THE CONVERSATION

Once you are familiar with the GROWTH framework and how it brings more shape to conversations, you will begin to feel more confident dancing around it and fast-tracking parts of the conversation in response to different circumstances. When your time is limited (as it often is in impromptu conversations), you may have good reason to help your partner cut to the chase, albeit in a sensitive and supportive manner. A further iteration of this agile approach to being an effective conversation leader in very brief conversations is to be guided by the following three questions:

- What's wanted? (Goal) (and what else? ×2)
- What's working? (Resources) (and what else? ×2)
- What's next? (Tactics)

Even if you don't choose to ask these questions directly, they are helpful reminders of your intentions as the conversation progresses.

RA-RA CORRIDOR COACHING

Like most humans, conversation leaders generally appreciate having options from which to choose. RA-RA is a flexible, abbreviated framework proposed by Anthony Grant (2019) to facilitate "corridor coaching," his term for what we call "got a minute?" conversations.

The RA-RA framework:

- **R**ecognize (the opportunity for coaching to be helpful. Is this a coachable moment?)
- **A**sk (to clarify what's wanted)
- **R**eframe (with a clarifying paraphrase: "So what you seem to want is… is that right?")
- **A**gree (on next steps—and write them down)

ACE CONVERSATIONS

Here's a final acronym to help you confirm the effectiveness of your coaching approach conversations. Conversations that are ACE result in

- Actions
- Clarity
- Energy

Our conversations are as good as the impact they have. Action steps, however small, serve as a gauge of your partner's progress. You might think the conversation was positive; however, unless you can trace your conversation partner's progress across the action steps they have formulated, you won't be able to know whether the conversation has moved them forward in their thinking or practice.

Enhanced clarity is the second measure of effectiveness in the ACE framework. You may feel that you have greater clarity into your partner's thinking, but the real test is whether they have such clarity. You can test this by asking, "What has become clearer for you now?" Further, the best conversations should motivate your partner. A positive sign of this motivation is increased energy (the E in ACE)—something that you can often discern from your partner's tone, demeanor, or even their body language. One of the most satisfying signs of an uptick in energy is when they literally have a spring in their step!

BRINGING A COACHING WAY OF BEING IN THE MOMENT

Recall that a coaching way of being describes how we show up as an effective conversation leader. Unlike the skills (what you do) you might deploy, a way of being relates more to your presence (how you are) in a conversation. Chapter 7 provided an overview of the characteristics of a coaching way of being: humility and respect; belief in others, care, and empathy; integrity; cultural capability; confidence; and a solution-focused orientation. We proposed these as default components of a coaching approach to leading conversations, whether or not you have the luxury of time. You obviously can't preplan spontaneous conversations that you didn't initiate; however, in the following sections, we provide some general guidelines for how to show up and be present when such coachable moments surface.

BELIEF IN OTHERS, CARE, AND EMPATHY

If you've ever been approached by an agitated colleague while you were in midst of performing an urgent task, you can appreciate how challenging it can be to show up in ways that embody these characteristics when you have no time to prepare and you have conflicting priorities. Nonetheless, you might open the exchange by acknowledging the conversation partner's need and providing an emotional paraphrase that describes how they seem to be experiencing their situation right now. Noticing and naming emotions generally conveys empathy and caring.

Another possible opener that communicates empathy is a statement along the lines of "I can see this is quite pressing for you, and I want to support you. What would be most helpful from me right now?" In some situations, it can be tempting to jump into rescuer mode. Common phrases like "What can I do for you?" or "What can I do to help?" generally signal rescuing behavior and, like giving advice prematurely, diminish opportunities to support your partner's thinking and progress and, ultimately, lessen their potential to achieve a more desirable outcome. You can mitigate your rescuer tendencies by substituting phrases like "How can I best help you to think this through?" or "What do you need from me in this conversation to help you manage this?" These alternatives subtly convey a far more empowering message that signals your belief in your partner and allows them to take the wheel.

Leaders also convey empathy through attentiveness. You can demonstrate this in several ways, some of which are quite simple like the following:

- Silence and put away your phone.
- Adjust your seating position or location to be more open to the conversation.
- Move from the hallway to a quieter location.
- Take notes (with permission).
- Use a whiteboard or chart to map their situation (again, with their permission).

As simple as this all seems, you will have days when you are too preoccupied or distracted to be as attentive as you'd like to be, in which case, the best advice we can offer is to be honest. Your partner will inevitably pick up on fake displays of interest and attentiveness. The outcomes of such visible insincerity are an erosion of trust, a decreased level of psychological safety and a diminishment in the quality of the conversation. So, if your thoughts and emotions are consumed by a pressing deadline from your line manager or preparing for what promises to be a challenging school board meeting, gently inform your conversation partner that you are in the midst of attending to an urgent priority. Tell them that you want to give them your full attention, and propose a later meeting time.

HUMILITY AND RESPECT

Your authentic curiosity is an expression of humility and demonstration of respect for your partner as the expert in their world. As we described in Chapter 3, when you consciously set aside your knowledge, expertise, and experience and allow your partner to explore their own ideas first, you adopt a beginner's mind. Your curiosity will be apparent to your partner in the questions you ask, which sometimes can be quite surprising and often prompt new insights. But again, how can you demonstrate authentic curiosity when you are in the midst of fighting your own fires? When a colleague approaches you at an inopportune moment, you are more apt to rush toward a quick resolution or push for rapid progress. But, before giving in to such temptation, consider the potentially harmful consequences of moving too fast. In such instances, instead, you might tactfully suggest that the conversation is important enough to warrant additional time and provide an alternative to the "got a minute?" moment.

CONFIDENCE AND INTEGRITY

While the conversation partner always leads the topic in "got a minute?" exchanges, the conversation leader manages the conversation (in service of the other's thinking and progress). When you are confident in your own abilities as a conversation leader, you will respond with a conversation manager orientation even in these brief, unscheduled conversations. Because of their time constraints, shorter, other-initiated, informal conversations often need more intentional management. This includes being aware of and attending to some of the following:

- Recognizing if this is a coachable moment, or not.
- Clarifying expectations.
- Discerning the starting stance required—facilitative, dialogical, or directive.
- Initiating some form of contracting.
- Getting started in an efficient but respectful way.
- Responsively drawing on the key coaching skills to invite your conversation partner to explore the topic with you.
- Finishing the conversation with a clear way forward and intention to check in later.

Even in brief unplanned conversations, each of these serves to convey the leader's personal integrity and that of the conversation itself, which in turn builds trust.

CONTRACTING IN "GOT A MINUTE?" CONVERSATIONS

In formal coaching contexts, coaches establish explicit and formal guidelines with their coachees. Not only is such contracting invaluable for setting expectations, but we believe it is fundamental to an ethical coaching practice. Unfortunately, it is generally neither practical nor appropriate in shorter, informal and unplanned coaching-like conversations. Nevertheless, conversation leaders should work to establish clear understandings of expectations for any of these conversations. Some matters that are critical to address include the following:

- **Confidentiality**: "What we discuss here will not go beyond this room." (Name any context-specific exceptions.)
- **Time constraints**: "I have a meeting starting in 10 minutes, but let's see how we go now and decide what happens next then?"
- **Roles each person might take in the conversation**: "What if I ask some questions to help clarify your thinking on this?"
- **How any differences in power or status might be managed**: "This is not a review meeting, just a chance for you to think out loud on this topic."
- **The purpose and use of any notes taken during or after the conversation**: "I'm just taking some brief notes to help me keep track of our thinking. I'm happy to share them with you."
- **Supportive challenge**: "I might spot opportunities to supportively challenge your thinking. How much of that do you want me to do? OK, I'll make sure I flag when I'm about to put a challenge to you. How does that sound to you?"

A SOLUTION-FOCUSED ORIENTATION

Just because a conversation is brief and unplanned doesn't preclude it from being solution-focused. In these coachable moments, we maintain our bias toward positive possibility in the future rather than obsess over the problem and its causes in the past. The more we practice this approach, the more ingrained it becomes in us, and the more we notice it in the way others think. When our partner is stuck in problem talk, we use reframing and other coaching techniques to direct them toward solutions and positive outcomes. In fact, we would argue that holding a solution-focused orientation, as evidenced by the questions we ask and what we choose to emphasize and amplify from our partner's responses, is perhaps even more important in less formal than in more formal contexts.

AGILE USE OF THE KEY COACHING SKILLS IN THE MOMENT

Chapter 6 provided a deep dive into key skills of effective conversation leaders: Listening to Encourage Thinking; Asking Powerful Questions; Paraphrasing and Summarizing; Sharing Knowledge and Perspective; and Noticing. While these five key skills may seem deceptively simple, learning to deploy them in agile and responsive ways, especially when we are limited to brief informal conversations, is a complex undertaking. We can't anticipate or rehearse these "got a minute?" coachable moments, and this element of surprise can easily catch us off guard.

> *Coaching is a specific kind of conversation, full of intention; subtle and not so subtle shifts in perspective; carefully nuanced language; and acutely refined listening among things. (Campbell, 2016, p. 140)*

If you take the time to study and practice these skills—ideally, as part of formal coaching—you can more responsively apply them in dynamic coaching approach conversations that will lead to better outcomes. For now, we offer the following words of reassurance:

1. No one (including the most seasoned coaches) is ever perfect in the mastery and application of these skills.

2. Your way of being (i.e., how you show up for your conversation partner) will likely override any real (or imagined) deficiencies in coaching skills.

Rather than revisit each of the skills in turn, here we bring attention to specific applications of the skills that are especially important in transforming "got a minute?" encounters into learning conversations. When done well, you may notice a crispness, momentum, and efficiency in how these brief conversations progress.

FOCUSING THE CONVERSATION

In formal coaching conversations (often 30–60 minutes in length), we typically have more time for rapport building and social niceties before we invite our coachee to tell us what they would like to think about in the session. In contrast, in "got a minute?" conversations, our conversation partner will often jump straight to their situation, at times without even waiting for you to answer the "have you got a minute?" question! In such instances, you need to tune in quickly, ascertain your partner's immediate need, and get to the point promptly. Getting to the point does not mean cutting your partner off, rescuing them, or showering them with advice. Rather, you get to the point by responding in ways that quickly bring focus to the conversation. The most effective way to accomplish this is to call upon them to clarify and use summarizing techniques to confirm what's wanted. "What's wanted" can mean what they want from you right now, for example, a sounding board, a collaboration, an advice- or direction-giver, or an empathetic ear. It can also refer to their longer-term "want" (i.e., their desired outcome, their options, and the steps that mark progress).

The following questions can help bring focus to the conversation quickly:

- "Yes, I've got ____ minutes before I need to get ready for a meeting. Will that be long enough to help, as a start?"
- "What do you need from me in the time we have?"
- "What's the best way for us to use our time right now?"
- "What's most on your mind right now?"
- "OK, it sounds like there are a few things there… and… and…, which of those would it be best for us to think through right now?"
- "So, what you want is…? Is that right?"
- What would be a good outcome for you from this brief conversation?"

GETTING (UN)STUCK IN THE MIDDLE

Even the best conversation leaders must navigate unpredictability. As we have stated throughout this book, conversation trajectories aren't always linear paths through the stages of a framework. Imagine that after a promising start in which your partner quickly clarifies their situation, you notice they are stuck. Perhaps they keep circling around the same point and can't seem to move beyond it. Given the limited time available, you may feel pressure to jump to giving advice; however, you can also use the following strategies to help them get beyond their inertia:

- Notice the stuckness and bring it into the conversation: "I'm noticing that we keep revisiting that particular issue and you seem a bit stuck. Would that be fair to say?"
- Then it can be helpful to ask the question: "What would be the best question I could ask you right now to move this forward?"

Other powerful questions include the following:

- "If we swapped roles right now, what would you tell me to do?"
- And the classic "miracle question" that has origins in solutions-focused therapy: "Imagine you went to bed tonight and woke in the morning to discover that this issue had miraculously disappeared. What would be the first tiny signs that things were better? And what else would you notice? And what else? What would others notice?"

- "Wow! Wouldn't that be great? So, what might be a first tiny step toward some of that?"

There are, of course, other strategies to draw from but, based on your partner's responses and/or your own time constraints, you may want to take a pause to allow sufficient time for them to gain more clarity, in which case:

- You could suggest a break to think further and then make time to resume the conversation a few hours or a day later.
- If your conversation partner agrees to this, another excellent strategy is to pose a reflection question that they can ponder in the interim, such as "What is the real issue for you here?" The same question can also be used during a conversation in which your partner seems to be rambling or spiraling around multiple issues.

When your partner is struggling to make a decision or is hesitant to commit to an option because of a perceived lack of time, you can also challenge them with some targeted questions. (Note, again, that as with all challenging interventions, seek their permission first.) For example, "Can I be a bit challenging here?" or "Would you mind if I asked what might feel like a slightly challenging question here?")

- "What's the cost of not doing this (or making this decision) now?"
- "If you knew you couldn't fail, which path would you choose?"
- "What's the least amount of time you need to set aside to get started on this?"

If the impasse seems to be a blind spot or a knowledge or experience gap, you can also draw on the know-how continuum from Chapter 6:

- "When has there been a time in the past when you managed a similar situation successfully? What worked for you then?"
- "Who else do you know who does this well or has experience of this that could help? How could you utilize them?"
- "Would you like some thoughts and suggestions from me?"
- "What I've seen work in similar situations is…or…and sometimes…can be helpful."
- "What could any of those look like for you?"
- "Tell me more about that."

Finally, dialing up our strengths radar is particularly important when our conversation partner seems stuck or lacking in confidence. When you are offering in-the-moment affirming feedback by noticing and naming their strengths, they know that you believe in them.

GENERATING MOMENTUM

As we mentioned earlier in this chapter, when spontaneous, other-initiated conversations are managed well, they have a crispness and momentum to them. When you use some of your key skills with agility, you can generate a tempo or pace to the exchange that helps your partner think clearly and make progress even in a relatively short space of time. Described below are some particularly pertinent examples.

Managing time and, therefore, the shape of the conversation, is an important coaching skill. With practice, coaches can manage the time spent on divergent and convergent thinking phases of the conversation. They strategically apply frameworks and skills and provide the coachee sufficient time to think and progress to action steps. This is all feasible in a formal coaching context but more challenging in brief in-the-moment conversations. Noticing is an important key skill in relation to time. We need to notice not only the passing of time but also the state of our partner's thinking at any given time. When we sharpen our awareness of time, we can better make decisions about whether to expand the thinking further with another "what else?" prompt, for example, or press for more focus or precision as the time available draws to a close. Don't be shy about articulating this with a statement like "I'm just keeping an eye on our time here and want to help you make some progress. Should we see where we've got to and what's next?" You and your partner will both be better served by this approach than by blindly carrying on until time runs out and you both have to rush off to other duties. It's easy to be swept away by the current of the conversation, so it is important to remind yourself that it is part of your job to manage time. Your partner's "job," on the other hand, is to do their best thinking!

Summarizing and incisive questioning bring focus and precision to shorter conversations and serve to generate the momentum we mentioned earlier.

Tactical and tactful interrupting is sometimes necessary in these conversations just as it is, albeit less commonly, in formal coaching sessions where coaches generally try to adhere to the rule of yielding to the coachee when they are speaking. However, when a coachee is prone to talking for excessive periods of time or when their thinking veers off-course into tangents, coaches may have good reason to not abide by the yield rule and instead attempt to redirect the coachee's thinking. In our brief conversations, with practice, we can do this gently and respectfully. For example, when you notice that your conversation partner's thinking is running off course into tangents, you might use a subtle, nonverbal approach such as leaning in and using a gesture that communicates your desire to speak. In doing so, you create a space for redirecting your partner's attention back to the main thread of the conversation. Of course, you should always apologize for cutting in and emphasize that you are doing so in the interest of managing the conversation. For example, you might gently remind your partner of your time constraints ("So sorry, but I notice that we only have a few minutes left. Are you OK with moving forward?") or, after apologizing, invite them to pause and summarize where they are in relation to the issue that they themselves raised at the outset ("So, we've covered a bit of ground there. What's clearer for you at this point?" or "What are you thinking now, in relation to the issue?").

SCALING QUESTIONS

Scaling techniques are very useful tools in solution-focused practice and have proven very powerful in coaching. Likewise, conversation leaders can easily apply scaling to "got a minute?" conversations to advance a partner's thinking and progress toward a goal.

We can use a 1–10 scale to gauge our conversation partner's current reality and to explore the resources they might be able to access to move forward.

Step 1: Introduce the scale. "Thinking about a 1–10 scale, where a 10 is everything you've just described and a 1 is that there is nothing in place to support movement toward the goal, where would you put yourself on the scale?"

Note the choice of language here. We are not asking them to rank or score the availability of necessary resources, not themselves.

Step 2: Establish resources. Once your conversation partner identifies a number on the scale, ask, "What gets you that high and not lower?" or "Great, so what makes it a 6 and not lower?"

Conversation leaders who use scaling techniques avoid asking follow-up questions that reinforce perceived weaknesses rather than strengths and resources; for example, "Why did you assign such a low ranking to that?" or "Why have you put it at a 2?" These prompts bring undue attention to the least helpful resources and are likely to elicit detail of deficiencies rather than resources (e.g., "My teammates are unreliable, and I can't count on them to complete the task"). By asking questions that amplify what is working or already is in place, you are more likely to boost motivation and self-efficacy.

Step 3: Expand the resources. "And what else gets you up to a 6?" or "And what else is already in place to support this?"

When you use such seemingly counterintuitive questions, you direct your conversation partner to begin exploring additional resources beyond what they already named. Naming these resources helps build a stronger sense of self-efficacy, which fuels their motivation all the more.

Step 4: Move up the scale. We now move to envisioning movement up the scale closer to attainment of the goal. Some key questions help here:

- "So, in response to my question about how close you are to reaching your goal (the 10/10 we described), you put yourself at a 6 now [possibly summarize the reasons they are that high]. That's great progress; tell me what a 7 would look like."
- "So, you're at a 6 now [possibly summarize the reasons they cited]. What would a 7 look like?
- "What would one or two points closer to a 10 look like?"
- "What else would you be noticing at a 7?"

We intentionally use "look like" in this question to help steer our conversation partner toward describing what would be happening or what they'd be noticing just a little further up the scale (e.g., "I'd be seeing higher levels of engagement from the team during our weekly meetings"). When you ask such questions, you send a subtle reminder that most change happens incrementally and that small shifts are within your conversation partner's reach.

The next category of question is intended to move our partner to identifying concrete things they could do to achieve what they've just described:

- "What are some options that would help get you do that?"
- "What could you work on next to help you get to a 7?"
- "What could you do to make that a reality?"

Again, when you add some expanders, you prompt your partner to build clarity and detail around the possible ways forward: "What else could you do?" "And what else would move you to a 7?"

NOTICING: WHAT'S GOING ON FOR OUR PARTNER?

By now, you can appreciate the essential role of noticing in any coaching conversation. But in the context of brief, informal coachable moments, the skill of noticing is especially important. When you don't have the luxuries of time, privacy, or preparedness, you must quickly ascertain whether the opportunity (or, in some instances, distraction) is, in fact, a coachable moment. If it is (and assuming you have the "minute" they requested), you notice from their responses to your prompts where your conversation partner is situated in the GROWTH framework. You also notice the emotional subtext that surfaces in your conversation partner's verbal and nonverbal behavior patterns and respond constructively to it, especially when the conversation is about a recent emotionally charged event.

NOTICING: WHAT'S GOING ON FOR US?

When we focus so much attention on another person, we may lose sight of our own feelings, beliefs, and judgments as the conversation progresses. As we stressed earlier, self-knowledge or intrapersonal awareness is another important factor that will enhance your agility. Think about it: Have you ever felt impatient or annoyed with a student or colleague you felt wasn't "getting it" quickly enough? How might such impatience impede your ability to best support their thinking and progress? Similarly, when our own emotions are triggered in the heat of an impromptu conversation, we may not be able to elevate the moment to one that promotes growth of our partner.

We are all human! Even the most experienced coaches have these triggering moments. However, you can also learn to prevent (or recover from) such moments by continually self-monitoring and noticing your own internal state. Ask yourself questions like "What am I feeling?" "What am I thinking as I listen and engage in this conversation?" "How might my emotions in this moment interfere with my ability to best serve this person's thinking and progress?" And then, more critically, perhaps, "What things am I noticing within myself that would be useful to disclose to my conversation partner?"

While you may find it challenging to achieve an appropriate balance between internal and external noticing, especially in a spontaneous, other-initiated conversation, with time and practice, you will sharpen this skill. In other words, small steps!

DISCERNING WHEN ADVICE MIGHT BE NEEDED

As we have stressed, a conversation leader should only offer observations, suggestions, or perspective with permission from their conversation partner and usually only when all other possibilities have been exhausted. However, since these types of conversations typically take place within a short window, you may feel the need to accelerate a change. That is, as a responder to any in-the-moment conversation request, you will likely act more as an interventionist than you would in a longer, more formal coaching interaction. Part of noticing and discerning is realizing when someone does need a life jacket to keep them afloat (and maybe even to stop them from walking off the job). As the situation becomes less critical, you can always shift your stance and return to a more developmental conversation when they are safely treading water again.

We don't mean to suggest that this gives you a license to default back to being a serial advice giver. Even when under pressure, we can stay in a dialogical stance and, using provisional language, suggest (rather than give advice) and offer our suggestions with humility. Rather than trying to solve your partner's problem using language like "I think you need to…," you might direct them to a resource that will help them gain more perspective or understanding rather than immediately solving the problem. Or, you may help them accept that progress in the context of a brief hallway conversation might simply be to agree to take a bit of space to reflect and regroup (ideally, with more time and in a quieter setting).

Other-initiated, "got a minute?" conversations occur frequently in any given week. You will have days where you find yourself spending nearly all of your time responding to unplanned interactions, and it can be easy to think of these as endless-interruption days in which nothing of substance is accomplished. At such times, we encourage you to reframe your thinking. Instead of endlessly frustrating interruptions, you may begin to think of these incidents as transformative moments that lead not only to significant growth and progress for your colleagues and peers but, ultimately, serve to better the lives of all members of your education community including, of course, the students.

PUTTING IT INTO PRACTICE

The spontaneous nature of these "got a minute?" conversations makes them difficult to prepare for. However, while the content of each of these interactions will be different every time, it is possible to prepare the approach that you might take when an opportunity does arise.

For example, reflect on the following general questions about your approach and, as best as possible, keep them in mind before the unexpected happens.

- How might you respond if you get a "got a minute?" request and you don't have "a minute"?
- How might you explicitly deal with the matter of confidentiality and exceptions or limits to this?
- What does contracting in the moment sound like so that you and your conversation partner agree to proceed on that basis?
- How might you need to modify the physical environment?
- What might you do to manage distractions if you are deeply involved in another task when the "got-a-minute?" request emerges?
- What strategies or internal mantras can help you to be fully present?
- What strategies or internal mantras can help you manage your Advice Monster?

CHAPTER 9

Leader-Initiated Conversations: "Can We Chat?"

> *"A machine can be controlled. A living system can only be disturbed."*
> FRITJOF CAPRA AND PIER LUIGI LUISI (2014)

In our earlier discussion of the Learning Conversations Map, we described other-initiated conversations as those that are initiated by our conversation partner in the moment. In general, leaders begin such exchanges with a facilitative stance as their partner takes the lead in sharing their topic. Conversely, when leaders initiate learning conversations, they typically approach the conversation in a more leader-led way. That is, initially at least, there is more of their voice and agenda in the conversation.

This chapter explores these leader-initiated conversations. Notice that these conversations appear in the bottom portion of the map (see Figure 9.1), indicating that they are often enacted in less formal settings or outside of formal processes. They begin as more leader-led conversations since the leader has invited the conversation and is likely to suggest the topic or agenda. If these conversations are true learning conversations where the conversation partner has choice, then it follows that they will be best served by a dialogical or facilitative stance as the conversation progresses.

As you read this chapter, keep in mind an important point: These less formal, leader-initiated conversations are learning conversations. In some situations, such as addressing performance concerns (e.g., duty of care), leaders must give directives and enforce compliance with them, in which case they might maintain a directive stance for the duration of the conversation.

Initially at least, these conversations focus less on learning and more on correcting problematic behaviors. In the most extreme cases, these conversations are often guided by specific policies and formal processes. We would position these conversations off the Learning Conversations Map as indicated at the extreme right-hand end of Figure 9.1.

FIGURE 9.1
Leader-Initiated Conversations

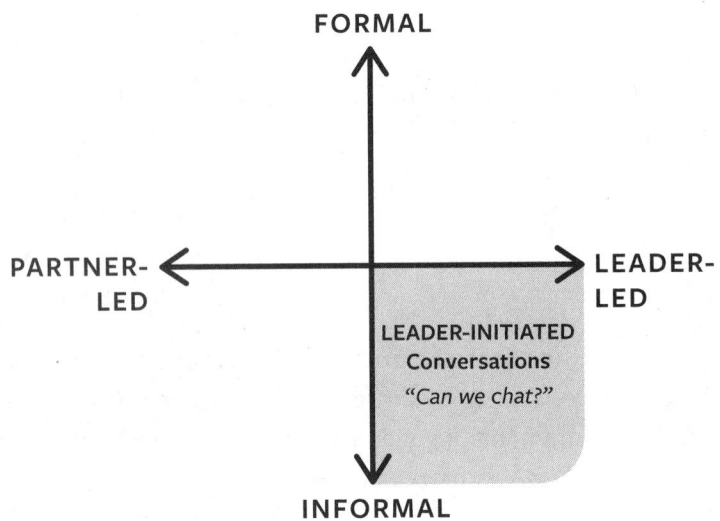

LEADER-INITIATED LEARNING CONVERSATIONS

Frequent leader-initiated learning conversations are a critically important way of supporting and maintaining collective efficacy across the organization. The leader who initiates these regular, and often brief, conversations routinely builds the capacity of those around them while advancing the strategic direction of the organization. As we shall see in this chapter, the subject of individual conversations may vary, but each of them shares some common functions, such as raising awareness, engendering responsibility, and supporting the progress of our conversation partner. Figure 9.2 indicates four broad purposes of these conversations (Checking In, Affirming Strengths and Resources, Areas for Development, and Clarifying Expectations), suggesting that, through dialogue, awareness is raised and responsibility encouraged, leading to progress.

FIGURE 9.2
Leader-Initiated Conversations

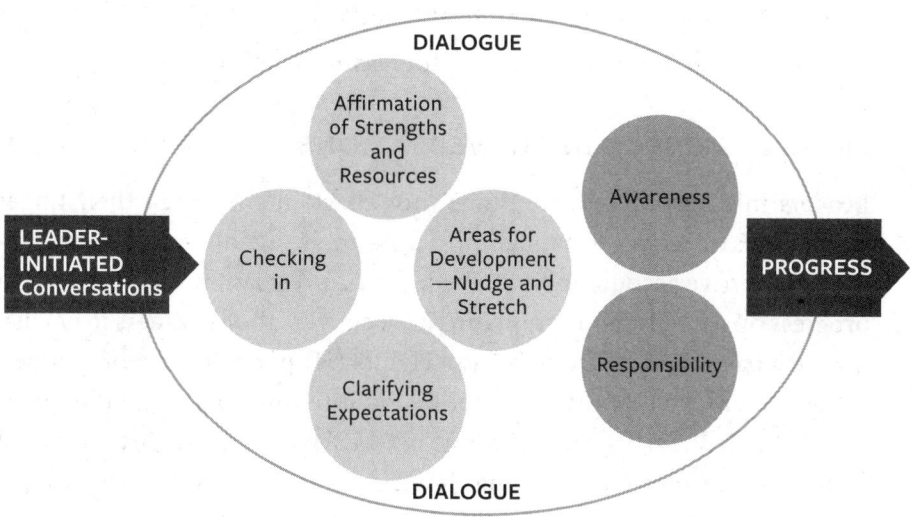

In Chapter 3, our introduction to the continuum, we described a dialogical stance as one in which leaders think together with their partners. Since *dialogue* is a term that is sometimes misunderstood, let us take a moment to consider the etymology of the word. In his seminal text, *On Dialogue*, David Bohm (1996) draws our attention to the word's origins in the Greek *dialogos*: *Dia*, meaning *through*; and *logos*, meaning *the word*. From this, we can understand dialogue as a stream of meaning flowing back and forth between two or more people in words. Critically, this is not the same as *discussion*. Bohm points out that the roots of the word *discussion* are the same as *percussion* and *concussion*, both of which imply breaking things up. As such, *discussion*, in Bohm's analysis, holds competitive, debate-like connotations in which the participants hold differing points of view and their goals are to win the competition and/or persuade their opponent that they are "right" (Bohm, 1996, p. 7). This is not the case in leader-initiated learning conversations. Rather than competing or winning, we are working toward shared meaning and progress.

Reflect on what it means to "think together" with another person. While the leader may choose to share their knowledge or perspective in the course of the dialogue, they do so in support of their partner's thinking and progress and frame their invitations accordingly. In such cases, invitations to enter into dialogue can be along the following lines:

- "Can we have a chat?"
- "I think we should meet to discuss…."
- "Are you open to me sharing some thoughts about…?"
- "Is this a good time to check in on progress with…?"

PROGRESS CHECK-IN CONVERSATIONS

Leaders initiate progress check-ins (not check-ups) to keep their finger on the pulse of what is happening across their organization and to provide supportive accountability to help their conversation partners sustain progress on agreed-upon actions. In these conversations, leaders may wish to touch base on the Tactics (T) and Habits (H) parts of previous conversations to ensure that their partner's good intentions translate into great results. We have all been in situations in which we had to modify our initial approach in response to changing circumstances. Leaders can use progress check-in conversations to help their partner think about such mid-course corrections.

Although leaders may initiate and lead significant development work in more formal meetings and longer collaborative sessions, they can also hold brief meetings to monitor progress after the initial work is done. Much as in the way we danced around the GROWTH framework to manage other-initiated conversations in Chapter 8, the acronym can bring shape to check-in conversations. The following series of questions describe a typical brief check-in conversation structure:

- "What's gone well since the last time we met?" (Reality/Resources)
- "What are some signs of progress?" or "What are you noticing?" (Goal)
- "On a scale of 1 to 10 in relation to your goal, where are you now?" (Reality)
- "What's got you to that point on the scale and not lower? What have you achieved?" (Resources)
- "What's one small step you will take to move one point further up the scale?" (Will/Tactics)

An even briefer example could use the G-R-T three-question framework from Chapter 8:

- **What's wanted?** "Last time we spoke, you were working on…. Is that still the goal?"

- **What's working?** "What are some signs of progress? What else are you noticing?"
- **What's next?** "What are you thinking you will do next? When will you do that?"

LET'S TALK ABOUT THE (OTHER) "F" WORD

Before we look at leader-initiated conversations that affirm, stretch and nudge, and clarify expectations, we feel the need to address the word that invariably comes up when leaders consider their need to initiate conversations—*feedback*. Feedback gets a bad rap! If we are honest with ourselves, the phrase "Can I give you some feedback" rarely fills us with eager anticipation. More often, we associate feedback with bad news or at least something judgmental, corrective, or deficit-based. Sadly, feedback is more often given or delivered than offered with an invitation to dialogue.

Before launching into these distinctions, take a moment to reflect on professional feedback you have received over the course of your career. What kind of feedback was most helpful? How was it delivered, by whom, and how did it help you?

Part of becoming an effective conversation leader is knowing which stance will best serve our partner's learning. In some cases, you might decide that taking a directive stance is the most expeditious way to effect change. With that said, as a leader, your purpose in initiating conversations is more often to enable greater insight and progress for your partner. We use the term "offering feedback" as opposed to "giving feedback" to describe this form of support and encourage a dialogical stance as the best way to maximize engagement with the information we offer.

Despite the negative associations that the word *feedback* may carry, not all feedback is judgmental or deficit-based. In the opening chapter of Douglas Stone and Sheila Heen's excellent book *Thanks for the Feedback* (2014), they pose the question "What counts as feedback?" and propose a reassuring and elegantly simple definition:

> *Feedback includes any information you get about yourself. In the broadest sense, it's how we learn about ourselves from our experiences and from other people—how we learn from life. (Stone & Heen, 2014, p. 4)*

If you reframe your definition of feedback as *information,* you are likely to find that your fears of being judged or "corrected" are diminished to some extent. The second part of Stone and Heen's definition makes an explicit link to the role of this information in supporting *learning.* At its essence, feedback is information that provides an additional perspective about a situation. This additional perspective may reinforce and strengthen current practice, or it can invite a change. When we take a coaching approach to offering feedback, we help people feel valued and hopeful so that they willingly take responsibility for doing something differently.

Have you ever captured video of yourself in the course of teaching a lesson or delivering a workshop? If so, think about how you felt when you summoned the courage to watch this footage. A common reaction is surprise: You saw something that you were entirely unaware of amidst the complexity and busyness of the situation. It is a simple truth (Knight, 2011) that most of us do not know what it looks like when we do what we do. For many of us, the surprise is also accompanied by regret or shame (a common lament is "Why didn't I notice that?"), but wouldn't it be more productive to reframe these experiences as opportunities for learning? The work of teaching and learning is complex, and when we are immersed in the process, it is difficult to have complete clarity about everything happening in our classrooms. This is all the more reason why, when a trusted other offers to provide information that will help to illuminate things that you may not have noticed or been aware of, accepting their offer not only can get you closer to achieving a goal but can also help you grow as a professional.

Positioning feedback as information that helps others to be more aware and, therefore, make more effective progress toward their goals should be key feature of a learning organization. However, all too often, this understanding of feedback is more aspirational than real. In many cases, what some call feedback is given (not offered) sporadically, inconsistently, and often confined to the context of formal performance appraisal processes. We don't dispute that multiple sources of feedback on our performance serve an important function in annual appraisals or more growth-orientated review and development processes (situated in the top-right quadrant of the Learning Conversations Map). However, when feedback is primarily limited to such formal contexts, recipients are more apt to think of it as judgmental and summative, similar to report cards. To counter this widespread experience, as leaders, we should make such information readily available and offer it frequently if we have a genuine desire to support the thinking and progress of other professionals.

HELPING THE INFORMATION LAND WELL

Regardless of the level of trust in your relationship with your conversation partner and how well prepared and objective you think you are, you need to have a high level of emotional intelligence and an understanding of how this allegedly helpful information is likely to land. In their book *Tell Me So I Can Hear You: A Developmental Approach to Feedback for Educators* (2016), Ellie Drago-Severson and Jessica Blum-DeStefano highlight three common challenges with feedback: a lack of good objective information, inconsistency in how it is provided, and a one-size-fits-all approach. They describe a developmental approach to feedback as "tuning the dial" for feedback recipients, all in the interest of expanding their capacity for meaning making. In the context of leader-initiated conversations, we strive to offer information that the recipient can hear, process, and make sense of.

A few considerations can guide you in accomplishing this.

What is it that I want to share?

- Data
- An observation
- A perspective or question

Why do I want to share this?

- To maintain progress
- To increase momentum
- To affirm strengths and draw attention to resources
- To suggest areas for development or growth
- To raise awareness of something that appears to be inhibiting progress

What's the best way to offer this information for this person?

- How does my conversation partner prefer to receive feedback?
- How are they likely to receive the invitation and information?
- How can I alleviate this?
- Is what I am sharing likely to trigger a strong reaction from my partner? Why?

As the leader offering feedback, what do I need to be aware of?

- What am I seeking by initiating this conversation?
- Do I have status or power over my conversation partner?
- How will I acknowledge this and mitigate it?
- Is my language objective and nonjudgmental?
- Do I genuinely want to engage in dialogue by inviting their perspective?

RESPECTFULLY SHARING INFORMATION

NOTICE AND NAME IT

In the course of your conversations, there are times when you will want to share observations with your conversation partner in the moment to help raise their awareness. As a simple mantra, "notice and name it" can be a helpful way of tuning our noticing to things that could be useful to our conversation partner. Sometimes this information will be about strengths and resources and at other times the opposite—about things that may be inhibiting their thinking and progress. Here are some examples:

How you experience your conversation partner:

- "Your enthusiasm and passion for…are really coming through in the way you at talking."
- "You seem really excited about that."
- "You seem a bit distracted today. I'm wondering if this is still a good time for you?"

Inconsistent nonverbal signals:

- "I'm noticing that your shoulders drop each time we appear to identify a way forward. What's going on there?"
- "I'm not seeing the usual level of energy from you today, and I'm wondering if there is something else that it would be helpful to talk about?"

Strong emotions:

- "That idea seems to have sparked a high level of enthusiasm and excitement in you."

- "Wow, I can really see that you are bursting with pride about that."
- "You seem quite frustrated by...."
- "You sound quite angry about...."

Patterns:

- "I'm noticing that you keep discrediting your own ideas just after you have suggested them, and I'm wondering what's driving that."
- "I've noticed that there seems to be a bit of a pattern developing where other things are preventing you from following through on the next steps we talked about. I'm wondering if the goal we're working on is still relevant."

When they model a goal area:

- "Wow! I think that is a great example of you hitting the collaboration instead of the collegiality part of your goal. Tell me more about how you did that."
- "The way you have just articulated what you'd like to see happen is a great example of that clarity of communication you've been aiming for with your team. I wonder if you have examples of when you have been able to do this with them."

AUTHENTIC AFFIRMING

Sadly, many of us don't receive or offer nearly enough positive, affirming feedback. When we receive praise statements like "well done" or "good job," we may feel affirmed (especially when given by people we respect). However, such generic statements don't usually help us understand specifically what we did well. Without this understanding, we are less likely to repeat the decisions or actions that earned the praise or to build on them. Experienced teachers know that the most valuable praise is explicitly linked to positive behaviors, routines, or actions that will advance their students' learning and, ultimately, serve them well in the future. Similarly, you can offer authentic affirming feedback that not only communicates your appreciation but also specifically names what you witnessed (or heard about) *and* the positive impact it had.

The best affirming feedback acknowledges a skill or quality in your conversation partner and highlights the positive difference it made in specific situations. When you add specificity to what you name, your conversation partner is more apt to retain it and less likely to brush it off or discount it. You not only help your conversation partner to feel more competent and be aware of and build upon their unique strengths, but the positive emotions the feedback evokes help fuel their sense of hope, self-efficacy, and resourcefulness.

Examples of authentic affirming:

- "Thank you for chairing the team meeting yesterday. I appreciated the way you used our agreed protocols to manage the time spent on each item. I noticed a greater level of positivity from the team as a result."
- "Based on what you just described, it seems like you now have a more sustainable study routine, and that helped boost your confidence during the debate."
- "I really appreciate the way you can summarize complex discussions into clear, actionable chunks. I saw you do this well in the planning session this morning, and it helped us all see what needs to be done."
- "I really appreciate your eye for detail. It has helped us to develop some really high-quality materials."
- "I appreciate the quality of your student report comments. Your specific comments both about their individual strengths and areas for development show that you really know each of your students."

NUDGE-AND-STRETCH FEEDBACK

When leaders consistently offer authentic affirming feedback to those around them, they enhance levels of trust. In the context of learning conversations, this trust helps your conversation partner to receive and respond constructively to more challenging feedback. Again, your goal as a leader is to stretch or "nudge" the thinking or practice of your conversation partner. We initiate these conversations by proposing an area or topic that we feel would support our partner's thinking to enhance their performance, well-being, or progress toward an agreed goal. For example, "May I share an observation that I think might help you prepare for next week's meeting?" When your partner begins to engage with your proposed topic or information, you can adopt a dialogical stance to help them make sense of this perspective and decide what they want to do with it.

A simple technique for sharing this kind of feedback is the feedback bridge. Many of us are familiar with the compliment-sandwich technique, which involves "sandwiching" negative feedback about someone's performance between two pieces of positive feedback. In truth, it rarely works. If you've ever been served such a sandwich, you most likely sensed the insincerity behind it. The attempt to disguise or soften what the person delivering it really wanted to tell you most often comes across as contrived. In contrast, the feedback bridge technique is a simple framework that supports the thinking of the conversation leader and invites constructive dialogue with their conversation partners. It is best used when you genuinely want to acknowledge and then stretch your conversation partner's practice.

STRUCTURE OF THE FEEDBACK BRIDGE

An affirming comment leads to a suggestion or stretch that builds on this strength, which leads to the reason(s) for the suggestion, which leads to an invitation for our partner's response. Figure 9.3 illustrates this process.

FIGURE 9.3
The Feedback Bridge

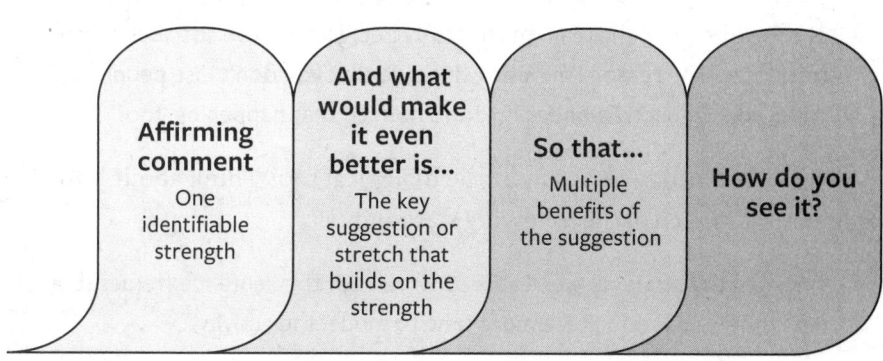

Notice the use of the word *and* in the second part of the statement. This is effectively the bridge between the initial affirming remark and the "even better" part. When we attempt to make these types of statements, many of us automatically use the word *but* in place of *and*. This seemingly subtle revision has significant impact on our partner's thinking, however. Rather than supporting our initial affirmation and building on our partner's thinking, the word *but* signals that something negative is about to follow, potentially prompting defensiveness and interfering with their ability to hear what we have to say. If you genuinely wish to support the learning and progress of your conversation partner, then the use of *and* should also be genuine. Here are some examples:

> "I really appreciate your expert content knowledge and the materials you produce for the students, and what would make it even better is if the delivery of the content could be more varied so that the students have more opportunities for collaboration and individual feedback. This would also allow them to engage with you and access your expertise in different ways. How do you see it?"

> "I'm really impressed with your ideas for developing the team, and I think this could be even better if you could develop a clear and concise plan for putting these ideas into practice so that you are clear on specific actions and timelines, and the team really benefits from this development. How do you see it?"

Or a variation:

> "I really appreciate the strategic thinking and big-picture vision that you bring to our Executive Team meetings—it's a real strength that underpins your contributions. I wanted to have a quick chat with you about yesterday's meeting because I think you could make more effective use of this strength in the team meetings by being a bit more succinct in your responses. The reason I'm raising this is so that you don't lose people and dilute your impact. I wonder if you've noticed that happening, too?

The feedback bridge serves as a true dialogical tool. Think about how you might react to each of the following statements:

> "Most of the students were able to work with the sentence frames, but next time you need to take more time to model the activity."

Or

> "The students seem to be much more comfortable explaining cause-and-effect relationships, and I think they might become even more comfortable if you try modeling the activity before starting the pair-share work."

If you prefer the second option, it is likely because it uses intentional language to suggest what's next, advocating the benefits of taking this approach and inviting dialogue. In contrast, the use of "you need to" in the first statement is more like a directive or order. Yet, as we have suggested elsewhere in this book, there may be times where such directive language, as part of a directive stance, is needed. For example, if you have an urgent matter to raise with your conversation partner, such as a concern about student safety in their classroom, or inappropriate behavior that you observed in a team meeting, we wouldn't advise trying to apply a dialogical framework. Even in cases that are not this extreme, a more direct approach is often warranted, as described in the following section.

CLARIFYING AND ALIGNING EXPECTATIONS: WHEN MORE THAN A NUDGE IS NEEDED

As much as we would like to envision schools in which we can assume a facilitative or dialogical stance in every conversation we lead, school leaders inevitably find themselves in situations where they must share clear and unambiguous information with their conversation partner, along with the suggestion of a modification in their behavior. When you engage in these directive conversations, your intent is to raise the awareness of your conversation partner, support them in understanding your perspective, and empower them to take responsibility for initiating change.

Again, these moments are quite distinct from conversations held in response to serious professional performance or behavior concerns. Such conversations are often referred to as hard, difficult, challenging, tough, and even fierce. As we have stated earlier, they would reside at the far right-hand end of the continuum we introduced in Chapter 3 and are depicted again in Figure 9.4. In most cases, you would best address the problematic behavior in a more formal setting where you can take the time you need to process it with your conversation partner and reach some resolution.

Often, the need for less extreme, more-than-a-nudge conversations arises out of misaligned expectations rather than serious malpractice. Typical examples include a lack of team contribution and follow-through on actions, a negative response to student feedback, a team member going off script from agreed curriculum content, or a pattern of lateness for staff meetings or submission of reports.

The figure in Figure 9.4 indicates the boundary point where you need to discern your level of directedness when expectations appear to be misaligned and you need to clarify agreed expectations with your conversation partner. At this point, the conversation needs to begin with a directive stance.

FIGURE 9.4
When More Than a Nudge Is Needed

Within supportive and trusting relationships, and against a backdrop of regular affirming and stretch feedback, these conversations need not be difficult. When positioned as learning conversations, such direct feedback comes from a place of support and is underpinned by the belief that your conversation partner has the capacity to change.

As leaders, we initiate these less formal concern-based conversations to draw attention to an issue in a timely manner so that it can be nipped in the bud before it becomes a bigger issue. When we share the concern, we need to be open to hearing what our partner has to say and be willing to shift our own perception of the situation in response, but at the same time be clear that choosing not to modify their behavior is not an option open to our conversation partner. Your partner may have choice in how they address the issue, and you may support them in thinking this through dialogically, but they cannot choose to keep submitting their reports past the agreed deadline, for example. A tension here is that if you are simply trying to prove that your own viewpoint is correct, you run the risk of generating an argument rather than a learning conversation. This is where a "third point" can be helpful, in the form of a reference to some objective data, an agreed-upon framework, or mutually agreed-upon expectations. Having a third point in the conversation helps mitigate the adversarial situation where we are each arguing for our point of view.

The most effective concern-based conversations have the following simple structure:

- Step 1: State your observations and how they link to agreed expectations.
- Step 2: Invite their response.
- Step 3: Emphasize ownership and importance, and loop back as necessary.
- Step 4: Once acknowledged, move to what's wanted instead and progress steps.

Here's an example:

Leader: Is now a good time for a chat about how our PLC meetings have been working? I've noticed that you've brought a pile of papers to grade during the last couple of meetings, and I'm concerned that you've not been fully present and able to contribute to the shared development work that we committed to as a group at the start of term.

I'm wondering what's going on for you?

Partner: I've been at all of the meetings that we agreed to. My marking has just been piling up a bit, and I needed to get the papers back to my students. They're a capable group anyway, and I don't have anything much to add.

Leader: I appreciate the challenge of keeping on top of your grading, especially at this time of year. I think we're all experiencing a bit of that right now. We do have a very capable team, and you are a valued member of that team. I want the team to benefit from your experience and expertise, and I know you have a lot to bring to the work.

I felt the need to raise this with you because we all committed to some team norms at the start of the year, and some of these were about our active participation in meetings and sharing the workload. I'm wondering how we can get back in alignment with those?

Partner: I know. I remember the discussion of the meeting norms, and I am happy to contribute to the work. It's just that right now, I'm putting my students first.

Leader: I really value how committed you are to supporting your students; I'd like to think we all are. The work we are doing in the PLC should be directly related to benefiting our students, too. I've noticed that other team members are also aware of your lack of participation, and I'm concerned that this could damage relationships as well as the productivity of the team if we don't address it. Remember, one of the norms we agreed to was that we would hold each other accountable to our commitments to the team. So, it would be good if we could consider ways of managing your grading and other duties so that you are able to be more present and active in the PLC meetings as agreed.

Partner: Oh look, I know we're all in the same boat and I'm not saying my work is more important than anyone else's. I wouldn't want to get off-side with any of the team. We all get along well. It might sound selfish, but I just find it hard to juggle everything.

Leader: I don't think it's selfish. You have high standards for yourself and your students, and I see this in your day-to-day work. I think this is about balance, and I'm keen to support you to work through it so that you can bring this to our PLC work too!

So, what could you do to make sure that you can be more present for our PLC meetings?

Partner: Well, I suppose I need to make them a higher priority ... To be honest, I often lose sight of the meetings, and when they come up in my daily calendar, they take me by surprise and I don't feel prepared. I know there's still a lot to juggle, but I suppose I need to see the PLC work as important, too.

Leader: I think the team would really appreciate that, and they would benefit from more contributions from you.

So, it sounds like one way to tackle this is to look a bit further ahead in your calendar and plan your workload to accommodate the PLC meetings. Is that right?

Partner: Yes, I think I need to try to do that.

Leader: OK, so if you plan ahead for active participation in the PLC meetings, what will that look like?

Partner: I think I need to highlight them in my calendar and maybe use the minutes of the meetings to remind me what we discussed and agreed. I plan chunks of time for my other work on a weekly basis, and I think I need to factor this in more consciously, too.

Leader: Great! And what will we notice at the PLC meetings as a result? What will you notice?

Partner: Well, I'll not have my papers to grade... and that means I'll be able to pay more attention and contribute. I am still keen to be part of this PLC, you know.

Leader: That's great to hear. OK, so what's your first step to make sure you can follow through on this?

Partner: The next meeting is in a few weeks, isn't it? That means I've got a bit of time to adjust things.

Leader: Yep, so what's a first small step you can take straight away to set yourself up for success?

Partner: Hmmm, well, I suppose it's going to my calendar this afternoon and rearranging my routine a bit. I might also have a look at our PLC documents and the team norms again as a bit of a reset.

Leader: Those sound like helpful first steps to me. How can I support you with this?

Partner: I'm not sure. It might be good to discuss my workload with you. Yes, and it would be good to revisit the norms at the next meeting for all of us too. That way it might not be so obvious that we've had this chat.

Leader: Sure, I can do that. How about we have a quick check-in conversation in a week to see how you're managing the adjustments?

This conversation is not a brief five-minute conversation that could be held in the hallway. Nonetheless, it is a fairly succinct leader-initiated interaction that could address the concern in, perhaps, 10–15 minutes. Be sure to check with your partner prior to the conversation to ensure that the meeting is scheduled for a mutually convenient time. As you read through the scenario again, notice the choice of language by the conversation leader, the third point of reference, the authentic affirming and acknowledging of the partner's responses, tactically letting some things go, looping back to the main issue, weaving in more compelling benefits of alignment, the point of acceptance, and the move to coaching. In this brief but important exchange, the conversation leader draws from their repertoire of key coaching skills, clearly exhibits a coaching way of being, and consequently is able to initiate and manage the conversation to a positive outcome.

AN ORIENTATION TOWARD ACTION AND PROGRESS

We initiate these conversations not only to share helpful information or perspectives but also to check in and drive progress. However brief, these interactions are key drivers of progress in complex human-intensive organizations like schools. Simply sharing information or giving our perspective is not enough.

The provision of information (aka feedback) that affirms, stretches, nudges, or clarifies expectations is only the first part of the equation. The presence of new information and enhanced levels of awareness does not automatically effect change. The gap between knowing and doing can be a difficult one to bridge. As illustrated in the example above, the skillful conversation leader supports their partner to move from awareness and acceptance to taking responsibility and acting.

IN CONCLUSION, YOU'VE GOT THIS!

After reading the last two chapters on being a conversation leader in less formal contexts, if you find yourself thinking that becoming effective is akin to preparing for an Olympic competition, this closing note is meant to provide reassurance. Sometimes, our way of being is even more important than our level of technical skill, so please don't feel compelled to memorize every sample prompt or response we included in this book. The best coaching questions are not on any list of powerful coaching questions (as helpful as these lists can sometimes be). Rather, the best questions respond to what your conversation partner has just said (or not said) and lead the conversation toward new insights and the actions toward the desired outcomes. The best response is an in-the-moment one that emerges from being fully present. Being fully present is also the root of skillful paraphrasing and summarizing and knowing when to offer such responses. A coaching way of being emerges from adopting a beginner's mind, from the courage to trust an instinct, and from a commitment to serve the best interests of your conversation partner. In short, if you are fully present, empathetic, humble, and caring in these conversations, then there is not a lot you can get wrong.

PUTTING IT INTO PRACTICE

This chapter may have challenged or expanded your understanding of the purposes of leader-initiated conversations and the nature of feedback. The following questions can serve as a helpful way of thinking about your response:

- **Start**: What do you need to start doing or do more of?
- **Stop**: What do you need to stop doing or do less of?
- **Continue**: What do you need to keep doing?

These are also useful questions to use when seeking feedback from others on your leadership team.

04
TAKING A WIDER AND LONGER VIEW

Chapter 10. Everyone a Conversation Leader:
              Toward a Coaching Culture

CHAPTER 10

Everyone a Conversation Leader: Toward a Coaching Culture

> *"Culture is nothing more than the accumulation of micro conversations."*
> HAESUN MOON (STANIER, 2023)

We wrote this book primarily for leaders in complex human-intensive systems. We believe that schools and other educational organizations are perfect examples of human-intensive systems, and we propose that a coaching way of leading is the best model for this context.

Our key principle is that we can lead through purposeful conversations where the conversation leader acts in ways that best serve the thinking and progress of those around them. We have called these *learning conversations* and developed the Learning Conversations Map as a way of thinking about the range of contexts for these interactions.

In this concluding chapter, we would like to widen the lens to consider the question—what if everyone was a better conversation leader?

To help you envision what this might look like in your setting, consider the following questions: Who, besides those in formal leadership positions, could lead these conversations? What are their conversational contexts, and where would these conversations sit on our map?

If conversations and the relationships they build are truly the lifeblood of schools, as we propose, then it follows that learning conversations can be enacted with a variety of stakeholders and across a variety of contexts. Consider how the interactions between teacher peers, teachers and parents/

caregivers, teachers and students, and even student to student all present the opportunity to be more purposefully led learning conversations. And, crucially, what would be the benefits to our education communities if we could enable more learning conversations like these? Could our proposed definition of leadership apply to anyone who engages in skillfully led, purposeful conversations? The Learning Conversations Map that was introduced in Chapter 4 primarily relates to those in formal leadership positions; however, we believe that the framework is applicable to a broader range of conversational contexts and participants, as depicted by the examples in Figure 10.1. These examples are not exhaustive and you may well identify other conversational contexts where a coaching approach could help.

Looking more broadly at the educational landscape, we know that coaching and coaching approaches have been applied in a range of contexts to support student and educator success and well-being. The Global Framework for Coaching and Mentoring in Education (van Nieuwerburgh et al., 2019) provides a way of thinking about how coaching, coaching approaches, and mentoring can make a positive difference in educational environments.

An adapted version of the Global Framework is shown in Figure 10.2. It depicts four "portals" that represent contexts or entry points (students, leaders, parents, and teachers) where coaching can enhance student success and well-being. Most of the chapters of this book focus on conversations from the perspective of the leadership portal, but when we take into account the variety of contexts that appear in our expanded Learning Conversations Map, it becomes clear how conversations have the potential to impact all of the portals. The wider range of conversation leaders in our education communities suggested in Figure 10.1 may work and impact more directly in one or more of the other portals as described above. This framework can be helpful in identifying potential starting points and contexts and the benefits we hope to see. For example:

To support **students** directly:

- Teachers with coaching skills are able to have more positive and solution-focused conversations with students.
- Teachers can use coaching to help students to build on their strengths, set inspiring goals, and increase their agency.
- Student coaching conversations elevate student voice and choice, enhancing student motivation and well-being.

- Training students to coach each other has been shown to have success and well-being benefits for both the students being coached and those doing the coaching.

FIGURE 10.1
Expanded Learning Conversations Map

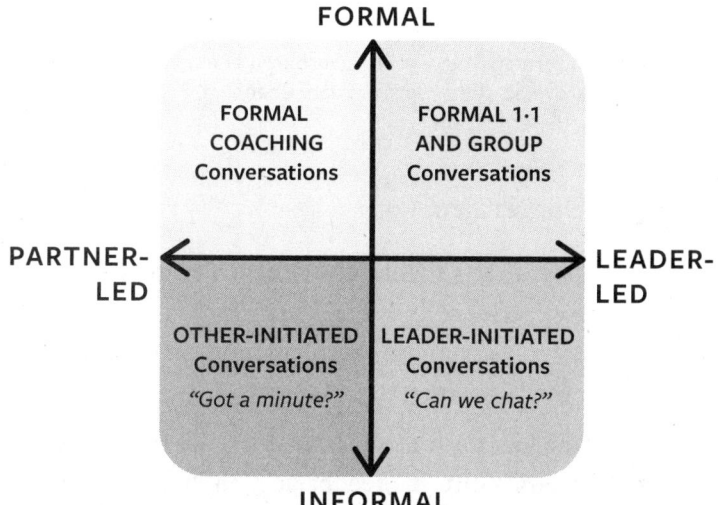

- Teacher-to-teacher peer observation and coaching cycles
- Teacher-to-student coaching
- Student-to-student coaching and mentoring
- Counselors and pastoral care leaders with students
- Support and administrative staff coaching and mentoring

- Teacher-to-student goal setting and progress meetings
- Parent-teacher interviews
- Specific needs reviews and IEP meetings
- Counselors and pastoral care leaders with students
- Educational support meetings
- Professional learning teams
- Support and administrative staff reviews

- Teacher peer support
- Student peer support
- Progress on projects and events
- Incidental student and parent interactions with staff
- Students with counselors and pastoral care leaders
- Support and administrative staff conversations

- Teacher to student
- Teacher to teacher
- Teacher to leader
- Support and administrative staff to each other and to manager
- Teacher-to-parent feedback
- Progress check-ins

FIGURE 10.2
The Global Framework for Coaching and Mentoring in Education

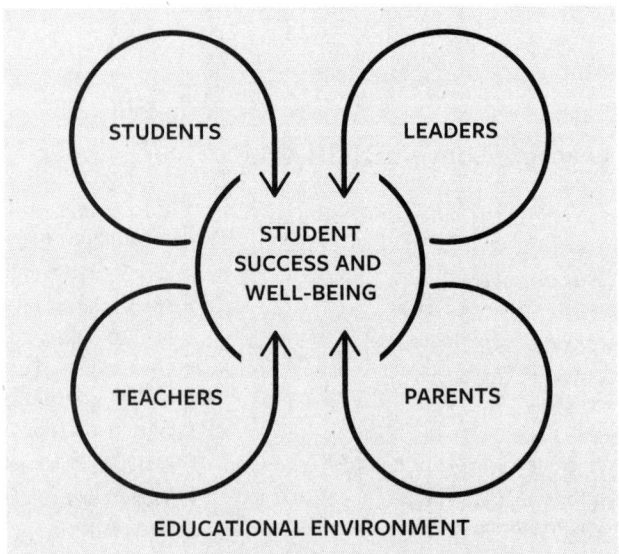

Source: Adapted from information in van Nieuwerburgh et al., 2019. In S. English, J. M. Sabatine, and P. Brownell (Eds.) *Professional Coaching: Principles and Practice* (pp. 411–426). Used with permission.

To support and develop teachers:

- Teachers and other educators who receive coaching related to their professional practice experience increased self-efficacy and exercise more agency so that they can sustain the implementation of new practices to meet the needs of their students.

- Teachers and other educators can use coaching skills to improve the quality of dialogue, including offering feedback, with their peers that leads to increased levels of collegiality, collaboration and trust.

To enhance communication and connection with parents and other community members:

- Teachers and leaders can deploy their coaching skills with parents, caregivers, and other members of the school community to increase levels of authentic engagement and collaboration.

- Teachers and leaders taking a coaching approach to communication with multiple stakeholders in their school community can increase their sense of commitment to and support for the aims and aspirations of the institution.

To support and develop leaders:

- Educational leaders who receive coaching benefit from having a safe space to reflect and plan, leading to greater strategic clarity, confidence, and agency.
- Educational leaders who adopt coaching as a way of leading are able to better support and engage their colleagues in a way that promotes ownership, responsibility, and professionalism.

TOWARD A COACHING CULTURE FOR LEARNING

The idea of a coaching culture, or coaching culture for learning (Munro et al., 2020), is an alluring yet somewhat fuzzy concept. Often, we find that leaders know something about coaching and would like to see a shift in the way their staff talk and relate to one another, but they are unclear about what this might look like or where to start. Typically, they make links to their prior knowledge of cultures of collaboration or feedback and to cultures of thinking, or perhaps they have specific conversational contexts or roles in mind. These are all reasonable starting points for the visioning process, and we have found that the following (coach-like) questions can help further develop your vision of a coaching culture.

- What does a "coaching culture" mean to you?
- What might it look like?
- What would be the signs? As it emerges? As it matures? Once it is embedded?
- If coaching (and a coaching approach) is the answer, what are the questions?

The final question about questions can help get to the heart of the change you want to see in your context. Examples—some specific, some general, and some grand—that we have heard in our consultancy work with schools include the following:

- How do we make professional development more participative and empower teachers to make more discerning choices in their learning and development?

- How can we scale up and sustain the implementation of well-founded teaching strategies?
- How do we create more safe space to talk about and develop practice, and thus de-privatize classroom practice?
- How can we make classroom observation and feedback less judgmental and more personalized to the development goals of each teacher?
- What can we do to build a culture of enhanced professional practice where constructive feedback is sought, offered, and received more positively?
- How can we generate more progress-oriented team dialogue?
- What would support more positive and productive review and development conversations with staff?
- How can we enhance levels of collegiality and collaboration between staff?
- What kinds of conversations are most likely to enhance student success and well-being?
- How can we build our students' capacity for peer leadership?
- How can we lead more agency-enabling conversations with students?
- How can we ensure that parents feel better listened to and more involved in their children's learning?
- How can we enhance genuine partnership between parents and school?
- How can we make parent-teacher communication more dialogical?
- What would improve relationships and enhance engagement with school governors and boards?
- How can we build a high-performance culture that honors the professionalism of our educators and supports them to thrive in their roles?

The Putting It into Practice section at the end of this chapter is designed to help you think about your answers from the perspective of your own context.

DEFINING A COACHING CULTURE

In their review of the literature on coaching cultures in organizations, Gormley and van Nieuwerburgh (2014) concluded that such cultures hold the promise of more positive and supportive climates for personal and organizational growth. Building on this concept in relation to education contexts, Munro, Barr, and van Nieuwerburgh (2020) offer the following definition:

> A whole-school coaching culture for learning exists when education leaders, teachers, support staff, students, parents and other partners, intentionally use coaching and coaching approaches in a range of conversational contexts. For this to happen, coaching approaches should be widely understood and skilfully utilised across the school community. In such a culture, a coaching approach to conversations about learning will need to become part of an organisation's "way of being" with appropriate resourcing and explicit integration into the school's strategic plans. (p. 229)

Of course, as with most ambitious undertakings, we can't expect an entire culture to shift overnight. Our experience working with schools and other education organizations has led us to believe that the process of establishing a coaching culture is more akin to a journey than a destination. Its starting points and evolution are influenced by various contextual factors. We hope that the following questions will get you started on this journey.

- Who initiates the journey?
- What are the starting points?
- Has your school or organization positioned coaching authentically within its professional learning architecture?
- How do your accountability processes and management hierarchies influence the culture of your school/organization?
- What are antecedent conditions related to school culture and past experiences of staff that may facilitate (or impede) the establishment of a coaching culture?
- Does your school/organization provide advocacy for and leadership of coaching and coaching approaches?
- How will your organization work to develop and maintain coaching expertise?
- What are the signs of progress and growth that you expect to see over time?
- How will your strategic planning and resourcing serve to embed and sustain new ways of working?

STAGES OF DEVELOPMENT

In his book *Coaching in Professional Contexts* (2016), Christian van Nieuwerburgh proposes the ACTION acronym to represent the key stages in the establishment of a coaching culture (p. 232):

- Assessment
- Championing
- Training
- Internal Coaching Resource
- Organizational Alignment
- Normalization

Let's now look at how the ACTION framework would translate into the current discussion.

A. Typically, those who share an awareness of the benefits of coaching (often those who have been coached themselves) initiate the **assessment** phase, which is not unlike a feasibility study that is conducted prior to the commencement of a substantial undertaking. Questions that follow might include "How well is the organization doing already?" "What is in place?" "What is the appetite for coaching and coaching approaches?" "Who will support it?" "How will leadership buy-in be secured?"

C. This initial stage may be followed by some **championing**. For example, we might enlist the support of influential leaders who are enthusiastic about the proposed coaching culture and who will champion the benefits of coaching, particularly by modeling best practice and getting involved in coaching initiatives.

T. We can't overemphasize the value of **high-quality training** for those who will be involved in coaching and/or adopt a coaching approach with others. Admittedly, as leaders in an organization that provides this kind of training, we are somewhat biased. However, the maxim "we act our way into learning," rather than "we learn our way into acting," holds true here. We hope that the experience, knowledge, and evidence we have poured into this book will take you far, but you can maximize your learning if you engage in formal training with expert practitioners who can bring our concepts to life and hold a safe space in which you can learn alongside others.

I. Many otherwise promising initiatives don't succeed over time because of inadequate planning for sustainability. For this reason, we also recommend forming ongoing support mechanisms, such as communities of practice, to sustain an **internal coaching resource**. Indeed, the existence of internal coaches seems to be one of the principal ways of leveraging the benefits of coaching within professional contexts (Gormley & van Nieuwerburgh, 2014).

O. Further, a key to the long-term success of coaching in educational and other contexts is **organizational alignment**. Coaching should not be framed as a bolt-on initiative; rather, "a coaching way of being" should inform each of our initiatives and, more generally, our interpersonal interactions.

N. According to van Nieuwerburgh (2016), the final stage necessary for embedding coaching within organizations is **normalization**. At this point, coaching is simply part of the way we do things around here. In schools, we observe it in both formal and informal conversations between leaders and teachers, teachers and their peers, teachers and students, and, in the best cases, students and their peers.

IMPLEMENTATION

We are not fans of the word *implementation* when applied to the context of developing a coaching culture. Instead, we prefer terms like *emergence* and *evolution*, which we believe are more accurate descriptors of what is unquestionably a complex developmental process. As is the case with teaching, in complex human-intensive systems, we don't pretend to have a one-size-fits-all approach that guarantees success. Nevertheless, we can point to some indicators of organizational alignment and normalization of coaching interventions (van Nieuwerburgh, 2016, p. 232) that we would expect to see when a coaching culture starts to become our default (adapted from Munro et al., 2020, p. 244):

- Coaching is no longer viewed as an initiative—it's just how we do things now.
- Common coaching language and principles are apparent in a wide range of conversational contexts.
- The members of our communities understand and have procedural clarity around the intent of different forms of coaching, from formal coaching to coaching-infused leadership approaches.

- Policies, strategic plans, and role descriptions reflect a common language and understanding of coaching approaches.
- Sustainable resourcing is in place to support an internal coaching resource.
- We intentionally apply coaching and coaching approaches across all four portals of the Global Framework depicted in Figure 10.2.

IN CONCLUSION

We hope that, having read this book, you share our desire to act to establish a coaching culture in your school or organization. We probably don't need to convince you that the brilliance of teachers (or school leaders, for that matter) is too often overlooked by the media and society at large. We believe that the vast majority of educators are fantastic learners who share a common desire to positively impact the lives of the children they serve. A coaching culture, and the coaching way of leading that underpins it, is one that values educators' autonomy and choice based on the belief that they are thinking professionals striving to do the best they can for their students and the community to which they belong.

Returning to our central theme throughout this book, intentional and purposeful conversations are the medium through which leadership is enacted and culture is shaped in human-intensive systems like schools. Regardless of organizational structure or prevailing policy framework, influence, learning, and progress happen through conversation. Fundamentally, change and progress will be enabled or inhibited by how we talk and what we talk about.

PUTTING IT INTO PRACTICE

The following questions can be used to coach yourself or to work with a team to clarify what a coaching culture could mean in your contexts. Equally, these typical coaching questions could be used when exploring any change initiative.

- **Starting points and contexts:** Thinking about the conversational contexts around the Global Framework (Figure 10.2), where do you see coaching and coaching approaches being most helpful first in the context of your role or work?

- **The "why"**: So, if coaching is the answer in this context, what is the question?
- **Your preferred future**: Imagine that 6–12 months from now, coaching or a coaching approach is making the positive difference you are hoping for. What will you be noticing? What would that look/sound/feel like, precisely? And what will that get you? What will teachers be noticing? What will leaders be noticing? What about students, parents, or the community?
- **Looking for resources (past)**: In the past, what has helped support changes that involved new ways of doing things in your context?
- **Looking for resources (present)**: What's already working or in place that can support the introduction of coaching and a coaching approach in your context? What makes these things work well? What else?
- **Scaling reality**: On a scale of 1–10, where 10 is what you have described as your preferred future and 1 is that there is nothing already happening to support this, where are you now?
- **Moving up the scale**: What are three things you could do this term to move one or two points up this scale?
- **Setting up for success**: Who else needs to be involved?
- **Sustaining success**: What training or other resourcing is required to support this?

References

Amabile, T., & Kramer, S. (2011). *The progress principle: Using small wins to ignite joy, engagement and creativity at work.* Harvard Business Review Press.

Ancona, D. (2012). Sensemaking: Framing and acting in the unknown. In S. Snook, N. Nohria, & R. Khurana (Eds.), *The handbook for teaching leadership: Knowing, doing, and being* (pp. 9–13). Sage Publications.

Armstrong, H. (2012). Coaching as dialogue: Creating spaces for (mis)understandings. *International Journal of Evidence-Based Coaching and Mentoring,* 10(1), 33–47.

Bohm, D. (1996). *On dialogue.* Routledge.

Braunstein, K., & Grant, A. M. (2016). Approaching solutions or avoiding problems? The differential effects of approach and avoidance goals with solution-focused and problem-focused coaching questions. *Coaching: An International Journal of Theory, Research and Practice,* 9(2), 93–109. https://doi.org/10.1080/17521882.2016.1186705

Campbell, J. (2016a). Framework for practitioners 2: The GROWTH model. In C. van Nieuwerburgh (Ed.), *Coaching in professional contexts* (pp. 235–240). Sage.

Campbell, J. (2016b). Coaching in schools. In C. van Nieuwerburgh (Ed.), *Coaching in professional contexts* (pp. 131–143). Sage.

Campbell, J., & Pascoe, J. (2020). Exploring the leadership conversations map. *CollectivED Working Papers,* 11, 43-46. Leeds Beckett University, Carnegie School of Education.

Campbell, J., & van Nieuwerburgh, C. (2018). *The leader's guide to coaching in schools: Creating conditions for effective learning.* Corwin.

Capra, F., & Luisi, P. L. (2014). *The systems view of life: A unifying vision.* Cambridge University Press.

Cooperrider, D. L. (2018). Introduction. In J. M. Stavros & C. Torres, *Conversations worth having: Using appreciative inquiry to fuel productive and meaningful engagement* (pp. xv–xviii). Berrett-Koehler.

Cross, R., & Parker, A. (2004). *The hidden power of social networks: Understanding how work really gets done in organisations.* Harvard Business School Press.

Drago-Severson, E., & Blum-DeStefano, J. (2016). *Tell me so I can hear you: A developmental approach to feedback for educators.* Harvard Education Press.

Dutton, J. (2003). *How to energize your workplace: How to sustain high-quality connections at work.* Jossey-Bass.

Earley, J. W. (2019). *The common rule: Habits of purpose for an age of distraction.* InterVarsity Press.

Fairhurst, G., & Sarr, R. (1996). *The art of framing: Managing the language of leadership.* Jossey-Bass.

George, E., Iveson, C., & Ratner, H. (2012). *Solution focused brief therapy: 100 key points and techniques.* Routledge.

Glaser, J. (2014). *Conversational intelligence: How great leaders build trust & get extraordinary results.* Bibliomotion.

Goleman, D. (1995). *Emotional intelligence: Why it can matter more than IQ.* Bantam Books.

Gormley, H., & van Nieuwerburgh, C. (2014). Developing coaching cultures: a review of the literature. *Coaching: An International Journal of Theory, Research and Practice, 7*, 90–101.

Grant, A. H. (2019). RA-RA: A framework for corridor coaching. Conference presentation. 7th Coaching in Education Conference. Sydney, Australia.

Grant, A. M. (2012). An integrated model of goal-focused coaching: An evidence-based framework for teaching and practice. *International Coaching Psychology Review, 7*(2), 146–165. https://doi.org/10.53841/bpsicpr.2012.7.2.146

Groysberg, B., & Slind, M. (2012). *Talk Inc.: How trusted leaders use conversation to power their organisations.* Harvard Business Review Press.

Hargreaves, A., & Fullan, M. (2012). *Professional capital: Transforming teaching in every school.* Teachers College Press.

Hook, J. N., Davis, D. E., Owen, J., Worthington, E. L., Jr., & Utsey, S. O. (2013). Cultural humility: Measuring openness to culturally diverse clients. *Journal of Counseling Psychology, 60*(3), 353–366. https://doi.org/10.1037/a0032595

Hurley, T., & Brown, J. (2010). Conversational leadership: Thinking together for a change. *Oxford Leadership Journal, 1*(2), 1–9.

Jackson, P., & McKergow, M. (2011). *The solutions focus: Making coaching and change SIMPLE.* Nicholas Brealey.

Kegan, R., & Lahey, L. L. (2002). *How the way we talk can change the way we work: Seven languages for transformation.* Jossey-Bass.

Kelm, J. B. (2005). *Appreciative living: The principles of appreciative inquiry in personal life.* Venet Publishers.

Kline, N. (2011). *Time to think: Listening to ignite the human mind.* Octopus Publishing Group Ltd.

Knight, J. (2022). *The definitive guide to instructional coaching: Seven factors for success.* ASCD.

Knight, J. (2016). *Better conversations: Coaching ourselves and each other to be more credible, caring, and connected.* Corwin.

Knight, J. (2011). *Unmistakable Impact: A partnership approach for dramatically improving instruction.* Corwin.

Knight, N., & Hill, J. (2023). Cultural capability as a way of being in aoteroa New Zealand. *GCI Insights.* https://www.growthcoaching.com.au/resource/gci-insights-june-2023/

Lambert, L. (Ed.). (1995). *The constructivist leader.* Teachers College Press.

Lopez, S. (2013). *Making hope happen.* Free Press.

McDaniel, R. (2007). Management strategies for complex adaptive systems: Sensemaking, learning, and improvisation. *Performance Improvement Quarterly, 20*(2), 21–42.

McKergow, M. (2021). *The next generation of solution focused practice: Stretching the world for new opportunities and progress.* Routledge.

McKergow, M. (2009). Gathering know-how for improved performance. *Coaching at Work, 4*(3), 52.

Munro, C. (2022). *Engaging in professional conversations.* Paper prepared for the School Leadership Institute, NSW Department of Education, Sydney, Australia.

Munro, C. (2020). A continuum of professional learning conversations: Coaching, mentoring and everything in between. *CollectivED Working Papers,* 11, 37–42. Leeds Beckett University, Carnegie School of Education.

Munro, C., Barr, M., & van Nieuwerburgh, C. (2020). Creating coaching cultures in schools. In E. Jackson & A. Berkeley (Eds.) *Sustaining Depth and Meaning in School Leadership: Keeping Your Head* (pp. 226–245). Routledge.

Munro, C., & Campbell, J. (2022). Coaching as a way of leading. *Australian Educational Leader, 44*, Term 4. Australian Council for Educational Leaders.

Northouse, P. (2024). *Leadership: Theory and practice* (10th ed.). Sage Publications.

Reynolds, M. (2020). *Coach the person, not the problem: A guide to using reflective inquiry*. Berrett-Koehler Publishers.

Schein, E. H. (2009). *Helping: How to offer, give, and receive help*. Berrett-Koehler Publishers.

Schein, E. H. & Schein, P. A. (2021). *Humble inquiry: The gentle art of asking instead of telling*. Berrett-Koehler.

Stanier, M. B. (2023, August 15). From the vault: The doorway to shared meaning: Haesun Moon, author of 'Coaching: A to Z,' reads 'On Dialogue.' [Audio podcast episode]. MBS Works. https://www.2pageswithmbs.com/164-from-the-vault-the-doorway-to-shared-meaning-haesun-moon/

Stanier, M. B. (2020). *The advice trap: Be humble, stay curious & change the way you lead forever*. Box of Crayons Press.

Stanier, M. B. (2016). *The coaching habit: Say less, ask more and change the way you lead forever*. Box of Crayons Press.

Stavros, J. M., & Torres, C. B. (2018). *Conversations worth having: Using Appreciative Inquiry to fuel productive and meaningful engagement*. Berrett-Koehler Publishers.

Stone, D. & Heen, S. (2014). *Thanks for the feedback: The science and art of receiving feedback well*. Portfolio Penguin.

Sue, D. W., Sue, D., Neville, H. A., Smith, L. A. (2022). *Counseling the culturally diverse: Theory and practice* (9th ed.). Wiley.

van Nieuwerburgh, C. (2020). *An introduction to coaching skills: A practical guide*, 3rd ed. Sage

van Nieuwerburgh, C. (2016). Towards a coaching culture. In Christian van Nieuwerburgh (Ed.), *Coaching in Professional Contexts*. (pp. 227–234). Sage.

van Nieuwerburgh, C. (2012). *Coaching in education: Getting better results for students, educators and parents*. Karnac Books.

van Nieuwerburgh, C., Knight, J., & Campbell, J. (2019). Coaching in education. In S. English, J. M. Sabatine & P. Brownell (Eds.), *Professional coaching: Principles and practice*. (pp. 411–426). Springer.

Walker, R., & Aritz, J. (2014). *Leadership talk: A discourse approach to leader emergence.* Business Expert Press.

Wheatley, M. J. (2002). *Turning to one another: Simple conversations to restore hope to the future.* Berrett-Koehler Publishers.

Whitmore, J. (2009). *Coaching for performance: Growing human potential and purpose – The principles and practice of coaching and leadership* (4th ed.). Nicholas Brealey Publishing.

Wiseman, L. (2017). *Multipliers: How the best leaders make everyone smarter.* Harper Business.

INDEX

The letter *f* following a page locator denotes a figure.

accountability, questions provoking, 60
ACE conversations, 97–98
action, questions provoking, 60
ACTION framework for a coaching culture, 138–139
advice, 72–73, 109–110
affirming feedback, authentic, 119–120, 121*f*
agency, defined, 46
agency thinking, 46–47, 48*f*
agile thinking, 91–97, 101–102
approach goals, 45
attentiveness, 99
avoidance goals, 45
awareness of others, 76. *See also* noticing

beginner's mind, 21, 99
belief in others, 84, 98–99
bridging questions, 65

"can we chat?" *See* leader-initiated ("can we chat?") conversations
caring, 84, 98–99
change, customers for, 19
choice, partnership principle of, 82
clarifying skill, 62
coachable moments, 92
coaches
    ideal attributes of, 81
    partnership principles, 81–82
coaching
    formal, 27–29, 27*f*, 28*f*, 33–34
    GROWTH framework vs., 51
    sleeper skills of, 66–67

coaching—(*continued*)
    traditional, xiii
    as a way of leading, xiii–xiv, xvi*f*
coaching approach
    to conversations, 10–11
    Learning Conversations Map, 32
coaching conversations
    experimentation in, 15–16
    learning in, 14–15
    progress in, 16
    sensemaking in, 13–14
coaching culture, moving toward a, 135–140
a coaching way of being
    characteristic of, 82–86
    introduction, 80–82
    in the moment conversations, 98–100
    in other-initiated conversations, 98–100
    solutions-focused, 86–87
confidence, 85–86, 100
context in learning conversations
    formal, 27–29, 27*f*, 28*f*
    formal 1-1, 27*f*, 29–30, 30*f*
    formal vs. informal, 25–26, 26*f*, 27*f*
    group, 27*f*, 29–30, 30*f*
    leader-initiated, 27*f*, 30–31, 31*f*
    meaning of, 15
    other-initiated, 27*f*, 31–32, 32*f*
contracting, 33–34, 100–101
contributions, meaningful, 10
conversation leaders
    everyone as, 131–135, 133*f*, 134*f*
    practices of, 13–16, 18

conversation leaders—*(continued)*
   teachers as, 36–37
   term use, 20
conversation leader stances
   context in, 25
   dialogical, 20, 21f, 22–23, 47, 70–71, 113
   directive, 20, 21f, 23–24
   facilitative, 20, 21–22, 21f, 69–70, 72–73
   overview, 20–21, 21f
   purposes, 25
conversation partners, term use, 20
conversations
   "can we chat?" *see* leader-initiated ("can we chat?") conversations
   coaching, 13–16
   a coaching approach to, 10–11
   continuum of, 18–19, 19f
   desirable outcomes of well-led, 13–16
   divergent vs. convergent, 48
   got a minute? *see* other-initiated ("got a minute?") conversations
   partnering, 20, 21f
   partner-led. *see* partner-led conversations
   quality, importance of, 6–7
   telling, 20, 21f
   transactional, 3–4
conversation skills. *See also* listening
   advice, giving, 72–73
   asking powerful questions, 59–60
   clarifying, 62
   introduction, 53–54
   key skills checklist, 78–79f
   knowledge, sharing, 67–72, 79f
   listing, organizing, prioritizing, 66–67
   noticing, 74–76, 75f, 79f

conversation skills—*(continued)*
   paraphrasing, 62–64, 66–67, 78–79f
   perspective, sharing, 67–72, 79f
   problem-focused questions, reframing, 61–62, 63f
   questions, asking powerful, 59–60, 78f
   summarizing, 62, 65–67, 78–79f, 105
cultural capability in learning conversation leaders, 85
curiosity, 58–59, 83, 99–100

dialogical stance, 20, 21f, 47, 70–71
dialogue
   etymology, 113
   partnership principle of, 82
directive stance, 20, 21f
discerning, 73
discussion, etiology, 113
distal goals, 45

emotional paraphrase, 65–66
emotions, listening for, 57–58
empathy, 58, 84, 98–99
energy interactions, positive, 10–11
engagement, 10–11
equality partnership principle, 82
experimentation, learning conversations and a culture of, 15–16
exploratory thinking, 46–47

facilitative stance, 20, 21f, 69–70, 72–73
feedback, in "can we chat?" conversations
   authentic affirming, 119–120, 121f
   effective, 115–116
   expectations, clarifying and aligning, 123–127, 124f

feedback, in "can we chat?"
  conversations—(continued)
    helpful, 117–118
    notice and name it, 118–119
    nudge-and-stretch, 120–121
    respectful, 118–119
feedback bridge, 121–123, 121f
formal 1-1 conversations, 27f, 29–30, 30f
formal coaching
  by leaders, 33–34
  on The Learning Conversations Map, 27–29, 27f, 28f
  time requirements, 33
  transferable elements of, 32–33

Global Framework for Coaching and Mentoring in Education, 132, 134f
goals
  compelling, 10
  types of, 45
Goals phase, GROWTH framework, 42–44, 43f
"got a minute?" See other-initiated ("got a minute?") conversations
group conversations, 27f, 29–30, 30f
GROWTH conversations
  condensed form, 96–98
  linearity in, 93
  in seven minutes, 95–96
GROWTH framework
  coaching vs., 51
  condensed form (G-R-T) questions, 96–97
  introduction, 42
  loops, cycles, and flexibility when using, 42, 49–50, 93–96
  simplicity of the, 51
  trust in the, 43f, 50–51

GROWTH framework, elements of the
  Goals, 42–45, 43f
  Habits, 43f, 49
  Options, 43f, 46–47
  overview, 43f
  Reality, 43f, 45–46
  Tactics, 43f, 48–49
  Will, 43f, 47–48
Growth Talk flow chart, xvif

Habits phase, GROWTH framework, 43f, 49
here-and-now humility, 82–83
hope, enhancing, 46–47, 48f
human-intensive systems, 9–10, 12–13
humility, 59, 82–84, 99–100

information, sharing respectfully, 118–119
insincerity, 99
instructional coaches, 35–36
integrity, 84, 100
intentional powerful questions, 60
interrupting, tactical and tactful, 105–106

Know-How Continuum, 68, 69f
knowledge, sharing, 67–72, 79f

language, subtleties in supporting thinking and progress, 76–77
leader-initiated ("Can we chat?") conversations. See also feedback, in "can we chat?" conversations
  action and progress, orienting toward, 127–128
  in context, 27f
  in the continuum of conversations, 19f

leader-initiated ("Can we chat?") conversations—*(continued)*
    expectations, clarifying and aligning, 123–127, 124f
    formal 1-1, 27f, 29–30, 30f
    group, 27f, 29–30, 30f
    introduction, 111–114
    Leadership Map location, 112f
    on The Learning Conversations Map, 26f, 27f, 30–31, 31f
    progress check-ins, 114–115
    purposes, 112, 113f
leadership
    in human-intensive organizations, defined, 12
    partnership principles, 81–82
    through conversations, 12–16
leadership theory, 12
leaders of conversations, stances
    context in, 25
    dialogical, 20, 21f, 22–23, 47, 70–71, 113
    directive, 20, 21f, 23–24
    facilitative, 20, 21–22, 21f, 69–70, 72–73
    overview, 20–21, 21f
    purposes, 25
learning
    a coaching culture for, moving toward, 134f
    outcome of well-lead conversations, 14–15
learning conversation leaders
    everyone as, 131–135, 133f, 134f
    practices of, 13–16, 18
    teachers as, 36–37
    term use, 20
learning conversation leaders, characteristics of
    belief in others, 84, 98–99
    care, 84, 98–99

learning conversation leaders, characteristics of—*(continued)*
    confidence, 85–86, 100
    cultural capability, 85
    empathy, 84, 98–99
    humility, 82–84, 99–100
    integrity, 84, 100
    respect, 82–84, 99–100
learning conversations
    in the continuum of conversations, 19f
    defined, 18
    linearity, 49–50
    transactional conversations vs., 3–4
learning conversations, contexts of
    formal 1-1, 27f, 29–30, 30f
    formal coaching, 27–29, 27f, 28f
    group, 27f, 29–30, 30f
    leader-initiated, 27f, 30–31, 31f
    other-initiated, 27f, 31–32, 32f
Learning Conversations Map
    axes and quadrants, 25–26, 26f
    contexts on the, 27f
    expanded, 133f
    formal 1-1 conversations, 27f, 29–30, 30f
    formal coaching conversations, 27–29, 27f, 28f
    group conversations, 27f, 29–30, 30f
    leader-initiated conversations, 27f, 30–31, 31f
    other-initiated conversations, 27f, 31–32, 32f
    using the, 32
Learning Conversations Map, role perspectives
    district leaders, 33–34
    instructional coaches, 35–36
    middle leaders, 34–35
    principals, 33–34

Learning Conversations Map, role perspectives—(continued)
   teachers as conversation leaders, 36–37
learning goals, 45
listening
   with curiosity, 58–59
   for emotions, 57–58
   with empathy, 58
   to encourage thinking, 54–55, 78f
   with humility, 59
   key skills checklist, 78f
   for resources, 57
   with respect, 59
   for strengths, 57
   tuning our, 55–56
   for what's wanted, 56–57
listening radar, 55–56
listing, organizing, and prioritizing in conversations, 66–67

multiplier leaders, 15

next practices, 14
notice and name it feedback, 118–119
noticing, 73–76, 75f, 79f, 108–109
nudge-and-stretch feedback, 120–121

1-1 conversations, formal, 27f, 29–30, 30f
Options phase, GROWTH framework, 43f, 46–47
other-initiated ("got a minute?") conversations
   advice, discerning when needed, 109–110
   agile thinking in, 91–97, 101–102
   a coaching way of being in, 98–100
   in context, 27f, 32f

other-initiated ("got a minute?") conversations—(continued)
   contracting in, 100–101
   focusing in, 96–97, 102–103
   generating momentum, 105–106
   getting (un)stuck, 103–105
   interrupting, tactical and tactful, 105–106
   learning conversations contexts, 31–32
   on The Learning Conversations Map, 92f
   noticing in, 105, 108–109
   questioning, incisive, 105
   scaling questions, 106–108
   shaping, 105
   solution-focused orientation, 101–105
   summarizing in, 105
   time, managing, 105
other-initiated ("got a minute?") conversations, characteristics of a coaching way of being in
   belief in others, 98–99
   care, 98–99
   confidence, 100
   empathy, 98–99
   humility, 99–100
   integrity, 100
   respect, 99–100

paraphrasing, 62–64, 66–67, 78–79f
parrot-phrasing, 64
partner-led conversations
   in the continuum of conversations, 19f
   formal coaching conversations, 27–29, 28f
   on The Learning Conversations Map, 26f, 27f
partnership principles, 81–82

partners of conversations, term use, 20
pathways thinking, 47, 48f
performance goals, 45
perspective, sharing, 67–72, 79f
praxis, partnership principle of, 82
preferred future. *See* goals
progress
    check-ins for, 114–115
    conversation leaders support of, 16
    a perception of, 10
    subtleties of language in supporting, 76–77
proximal goals, 45

questions
    asking powerful, 59–60, 78f
    getting (un)stuck, 103–105
    incisive, 105
    key skills checklist, 78f
    problem-focused, reframing, 61–62, 63f
    scaling, 106–108
    as tools of objective reality, 76
    "why?" 77

RA-RA corridor coaching, 97
reality, words in shaping, 76–77
Reality phase GROWTH framework, 43f, 45–46
real powerful questions, 60
reciprocity partnership principle, 82
reflection partnership principle, 82
reframing, 44, 86–87, 93–95, 116
rescuing behavior, 98–99
Resources, GROWTH framework, 45–46
resources, listening for, 57
respect, 59, 82–84, 99–100, 118–119
responsive powerful questions, 60

school leaders
    end-of-day reflections, 3–6
    role perspectives, 33–34
schools
    as human-intensive systems, 9–10
    as social networks, 10–11
self-awareness, noticing and, 76
self-concordant goals, 45
self-reflection, end-of-day, 3–6
sensemaking, conversation leaders and, 13–14
social constructionist theories, 76
social networks, schools as, 10–11
solutions-focused
    asking "why," 77
    a coaching way of being, 86–87
    "got a minute" conversations, 101–105
    powerful questions, 60
solutions-focused (SF) theory, 42–43
stances
    dialogical, 113
stances, conversation leaders
    context in, 25
    defined, 20, 80
    dialogical, 20, 21f, 22–23, 47, 70–71, 113
    directive, 20, 21f, 23–24
    facilitative, 20, 21–22, 21f, 69–70, 72–73
    overview, 20–21, 21f
    purposes, 25
    what-we-do part of, 80
strengths, listening for, 57
success
    belief in, 10
    sustaining, 49
succinct powerful questions, 60
summarizing
    conversation skills, 62, 65–67

summarizing—*(continued)*
   "got a Minute" conversations, 105
   key skills checklist, 78–79f

Tactics phase, GROWTH framework, 43f, 48–49
task enabling, 11
teachers as conversation leaders, 36–37
thinking
   listening to encourage, 54–55, 78f
   subtleties of language in supporting, 76–77

thinking together, 113–114
thought-provoking powerful questions, 60
time, managing, 105
trust, 43f, 50–51, 60

voice, partnership principle of, 82

what's wanted, listening for, 56–57
"why?" asking, 77
Will phase, GROWTH framework, 43f, 47–48
words, creating worlds and realities, 76–77

About the Authors

Chris Munro is now the Chief Operating Officer for the Australasian operations of Instructional Coaching Group (ICG) and Growth Coaching International (GCI)—both world-leading organisations in the field of coaching in education, now merged. He describes his role as supporting others as they grapple with the intersection of strategy, leadership, learning and relationships—helping them make progress, one conversation at a time.

Chris has held various teaching and educational leadership roles since qualifying as a high school design and technology teacher in the early 1990s. Relocating from Scotland to Australia in 2010, his experience and passion for people development coalesced with discovering coaching.

Chris credits early professional learning experiences with Jim Knight and John Campbell with helping him find the "thing" that would shape the rest of his career as an adult educator—coaching.

Chris is an accredited Senior Practitioner with the European Mentoring and Coaching Council (EMCC Global), holds a master's degree in social and educational research from the University of Aberdeen, and is a fellow of the Australian Council for Educational Leaders (Victoria).

Chris has presented at major conferences in the United Kingdom, Australia, New Zealand, Asia, and the United States.

John Campbell is the founding director of Growth Coaching International (GCI). This organization provides coaching and coaching services to educators across Australia.

John has been a high school teacher, a curriculum development advisor, and a management consultant in the corporate sector. Since 2004, John has led the GCI work across Australia, and more than 80,000 school leaders have participated in GCI professional learning programs.

He has coauthored several books and articles in the coaching in education field, and he has spoken at events and conferences across Australia, Asia, the United States, the Middle East, and the United Kingdom.

In addition to his teaching degree, he holds master's degrees in organizational communication and coaching psychology. He is currently completing a doctorate at Creighton University.

He splits his time between Sydney, Australia, and Bend, Oregon.

DON'T MISS A SINGLE ISSUE OF THIS AWARD-WINNING MAGAZINE.

iste+ascd
educational leadership

If you belong to a Professional Learning Community, you may be looking for a way to get your fellow educators' minds around a complex topic. Why not delve into a relevant theme issue of *Educational Leadership*, the journal written by educators for educators?

Subscribe now and browse or purchase back issues of our flagship publication at **www.ascd.org/el**. Discounts on bulk purchases are available.

iste+ascd

Arlington, VA USA
1-800-933-2723

www.ascd.org
www.iste.org